This Is
How You
Say Goodbye

This Is
How You
Say Goodbye

a daughter's memoir

Victoria Loustalot

St. Martin's Press
New York

Note to the Reader: The names of a few individuals depicted herein have been changed. Rest assured, however, that the names "Joe Pesci" and "Wolfgang" couldn't be more genuine. You truly can't make this stuff up.

THIS IS HOW YOU SAY GOODBYE. Copyright © 2013 by Victoria Loustalot. All rights reserved. Printed in the United States of America. For information, address St. Martin's Press, 175 Fifth Avenue, New York, N.Y. 10010.

www.stmartins.com

Library of Congress Cataloging-in-Publication Data

Loustalot, Victoria.
    This is how you say goodbye : a daughter's memoir / Victoria Loustalot. — First edition.
        pages cm
    ISBN 978-1-250-00520-5 (hardcover)
    ISBN 978-1-250-03866-1 (e-book)
    1. Loustalot, Victoria—Family.   2. Journalists—United States—Biography.   3. Children of AIDS patients.   I. Title.
    PN4874.L675A3 2013
    070.92—dc23
    [B]

                                                    2013013490

St. Martin's Press books may be purchased for educational, business, or promotional use. For information on bulk purchases, please contact Macmillan Corporate and Premium Sales Department at 1-800-221-7945, extension 5442, or write specialmarkets@macmillan.com.

First Edition: September 2013

10 9 8 7 6 5 4 3 2 1

For my mother,
night-light of my life

Grief starts to become indulgent, and it doesn't serve anyone, and it's painful. But if you transform it into remembrance, then you're magnifying the person you lost and also giving something of that person to other people, so they can experience something of that person.

—PATTI SMITH, October 14, 2011,
The New York Times

Victoria, mysterious child,
Mix of my blood
Will you turn out as wild?

—LOUIS LOUSTALOT, winter 1996,
as scrawled on a piece of scrap paper

This Is
How You
Say Goodbye

1

IT TOOK ME A LONG TIME TO LEARN HOW TO smile. I was never a child who could light up on command, who could give the photographer that open-mouthed beam, the kid face scrunched up like an accordion. That kind of giddy joy didn't interest me. I wanted to smile like an adult— understated and careful, like I knew what was going on and had decided to smile anyway.

So I practiced. I'd stand in front of the mirror trying on smiles like hats. The wide, teeth-bared grin that made my cheeks hurt. The tight-lipped Mona Lisa sliver. Sometimes I'd combine the two: my lips pressed into each other, I'd stretch my mouth until my cheeks stuck out farther than my ears. But no one likes a closed-mouth smile. I once tried a half-fake smile (which was also a half-real frown), reasoning that a little genuine was better than none at all. Here, one corner of my mouth tipped down toward my chin while the other curled upward so slightly it might have been a shadow. It was a neat trick, but it was no smile. None of those efforts made me look happy. They made me look like I was trying too hard. In that way, they were all genuine.

I practiced my smiles at my father's house. My bedroom there looked like the room of a very lucky little girl: four-poster mahogany bed with a white comforter that puffed up like a marshmallow and not one pillow but four, a matching night-stand, and even a mahogany vanity with brass knobs and a mirror as tall as I was. It felt like a set and I used it primarily as a rehearsal space. It was at my mother's house that I really lived, with my clutter and my toys and my couch.

Neither of my parents wanted the living room couch when they separated. When my father moved out, he furnished his new home with a burgundy leather couch that would have been ideal for a psychiatrist's office. At six, I called it the shrink couch. My mother, on the other hand, bought a dainty cushionless settee. It evoked Edith Wharton and was about as comfortable as a park bench. I inherited their compromise, this long white couch ill-advised for most adults but which I kept in pristine condition. I also commandeered their glass coffee table and requested a large gold "A" and a doorbell for the hallway outside my bedroom, but my mother had to draw the line somewhere.

I wanted the perfect smile for my life at my mother's house, but until I got it I practiced only in front of the vanity at my father's. I practiced after school and in the *l'heure entre chien et loup*—the hour of sunset when it's just light enough to make out figures, but too dark to differentiate between dogs and wolves. I stole that phrase from my dad.

I started practicing my smile before kindergarten when I had no idea that my future held thirteen years of class photos. Picture day, at least at my elementary school, brought the pressure: outfits were chosen, faces were scrubbed, and hair was combed. After all, this was the picture on which you—and your mother—would be judged. The picture that would be tucked into holiday cards and wallets, that would end up in photo albums and on mantels, dressers, and nightstands.

I wore a dress with pink flowers for my first picture day. It looked like old-lady sofa upholstery and had one of those lacy bibs that were so popular in the early 1990s. I had been proud of the dress when my mother zipped me into it that morning. But at recess Joe Pesci—yes, that really was his name—ripped the lacy bib during an especially ruthless game of tag. I burst into tears and ran to my kindergarten teacher.

"It won't show in the photo," she said, "but your tears will."

Which only made me cry harder.

At Sacred Heart we got our pictures taken in the slippery-floored gymnasium beneath barred windows. The photographer set up his hot lights and black spindly equipment under one basketball hoop, and we lined up by grade under the other. When it was my turn, I sat down on the little stool in front of the foggy blue Olan Mills backdrop. The lace on the front of my dress was hanging by a floral thread, and it flapped in the breeze of the photographer's portable fan. My eyes were still red, and I needed to blow my nose, but I did my best to look happy. The photographer took a few snapshots, stopped. His head appeared from behind the camera. "Can't you smile?" he asked.

My teacher was wrong. When the photos arrived in the mail, it was clear that my dress was torn. The lace was intact and appropriately flouncy on one side, but it drooped in the middle of my chest, sagging lower and lower, until it fell down across my arm like a loose bandage. On the plus side, it distracted from my uneven haircut, which my mother later claimed must have been a trick of photography—just the illusion of a terrible bob. Between the dress and the hair, though, I doubt anyone ever noticed that instead of smiling, I'd just opened my mouth, showcasing the gap between my two front teeth.

I LOOK LIKE my father. I've got his eyes—open wide and blank, firm, unreadable, they offer an unidentifiable challenge to no one in particular. I've got his knock-knees, French nose, baby-sized ears, and heart-shaped lips. More often than not, my father would smile with his lips pressed together. I always knew that beneath them was a cutting remark.

My mother told me once that I walk like him.

"I walk like I drive," I replied.

"So did your father," she said. "Too fast."

It was true. We did everything too fast. We moved swiftly: gaze ahead, focused on our destination, determined to reach it without delay. A dark bar, the playground, or somebody's arms—it didn't matter. Things were done and people were seen, because they were *on the list*. School, work, driving, kissing, job, wife, boyfriend, child, college. This is how we lived, my father and I. We checked things off like our lives were one long grocery list: dozen eggs, carton of milk, first kiss, avocados, learn to drive, get married, Fig Newtons.

I got to New York City as fast as I could. At seven, I told my mother I was moving there shortly and that she could visit. It took me a little longer but not much. I made it at eighteen. I came for college, but once here, my degree felt like it was taking too long. So I graduated in three years and checked my undergraduate education off my list.

And now I was a twenty-three-year-old graduate student living in New York City trying to be a writer but mostly just faking it. It was March, but dark and cold like January. I was in my living room, which I had styled to resemble an urban American bachelor pad from the late 1940s. I had a boxy charcoal sofa and a set of bubble tumblers I'd swiped from a Fashion's Night Out party I hadn't even been invited to. It was a room I imagined Philip Marlowe would have liked, if he'd given a damn about decorating. I sat in it now holding a plastic cassette case. Its label was yellow and peeling, like something left over. Something forgotten. But it wasn't. Not once had I forgotten it. On the label, in my father's handwriting, were the words A DAY IN THE LIFE OF LOUIS LOUSTALOT. The letters were unmistakably his—square blocks in black ink. Each letter looked like a building and when strung together into words and sentences the effect was that of a city skyline on the page. The day in question was a day in 1973 when my father was twenty-one and studying in Stockholm. The tape was a Christmas gift to his family in Bakersfield, California. It was his first Christmas away from home. The forty-five-minute recording was my father's way of being there.

There's no reason for me to have kept the case. I had the tape digitized. It was a file on my iTunes. I didn't even own a tape player anymore. But when I decided to listen to the recording, I got out the cassette. I popped it open and looked at the tape. I kept returning to it. Searching. Wanting to understand.

I rarely listened to my father. My iTunes and iPod synchronized automatically, so that my father's voice was also on my iPod, and the last time I played this recording was an accident. It had been almost a year before. I was at the gym, and it was late, after two A.M., which is when I usually go. The desk attendant is pleasantly somnolent, my favorite elliptical machine is always free, and I like the stillness.

The tiny cleaning woman in a blue polo, the one with dark, deep-set eyes and a long flat braid, moved apace between the machines as I went back and forth, back and forth on the elliptical. My iPod was on shuffle. Madonna's "Like a Prayer" ended, and the scratchy static of the old tape came on. My dad. I didn't miss a step on the machine. Just kept going, nowhere. Moving in place. I hit "skip" and listened to an Eminem song instead.

But that March night, I wanted to hear his voice. I wanted to remember a time when my father could speak to me. I wanted to remember a time when he spoke to me so often I thought I could afford to tune him out.

I sat on the windowsill, which required a bit of a leap and a twist to get up onto. There was nothing graceful about getting up on that windowsill, and in fact, I banged my knee doing so. The dull pain lingered in such a way that I knew I would have a bruise in the morning. I bruise like bananas, easily. It was raining hard; I wished it wasn't. The rain felt cheesy, like a dark and stormy night.

But I knew rain. I grew up with it: winter in the Sacramento Valley means rain. In elementary school, my classmates and I prayed for rain days when the Valley streets would flood. A real rain day didn't happen very often, but when it did the streets disappeared—replaced by a river rushing over curbs and around corners and filling the neighborhood with the singular smell of wet sidewalk. My friends and I ran out into the middle of the street not worrying about traffic because cars couldn't swim. We stomped around in rubber boots not because they kept our feet dry (they didn't) but because they made our feet bigger and stronger and created more powerful waves. We didn't care about getting soaked. It tickled us. Our hair stuck to our necks, our shirts to our chests—the water made us thicker, more substantial.

My father hated the rain. He hated the cold. In his dreams, he was a San Diego man.

I pressed "play." The familiar static, then music. I always forgot about the music. It was an upbeat song heavy with guitar—something you might dance to—but the recording was poor, and I couldn't decipher the lyrics. A minute later, the music cut out and my father's nasal voice filled my tiny living room. He was putting on an ironic voice, one that reminded me of Garrison Keillor. Though, of course, in 1973 the only people who had heard Garrison Keillor lived in Minnesota. My father sounded young, painfully young. He was twenty-one. Just two years younger than I was now. More than thirty years between us. But the way I heard him, he sounded as though he was right beside me, whispering in my ear. Only he didn't sound like the twenty-something boys I knew—the ones who leaned in so close they left warm traces of beer on my earlobe. Because it was impossible to listen to my father's voice at twenty-one and not know the things ahead. To not know the way his story ended.

Welcome to the Days of Our Lives. Today we're going to do a Day in the Life of Louis Loustalot. I know you'll all enjoy that . . . You're about to experience the ultimate in boredom. Not only do you get to watch homemade slides, but you get to listen to me at the same time. And I bet you thought you could get rid of me. (*Chuckles*) Teach you to think that. Somehow I have the confidence to know that you won't turn it off no matter how boring it is because it was made by me. (*Chuckles*) . . . Every time you hear this sound (*a bell rings*) that will mean to change slides just like in good old grammar school. Okay, let us begin. The first slide . . .

I didn't recognize the voice on the recording; I never did. I believed it was my father because I had been told it was, and it must have been, but this voice was light, carefree, and teasing.

He talked about the outside of his apartment in Stockholm; he lived on the "crappy side of the building where it was drab." Every morning he did laps around a track next door and, after, he relaxed in a sauna in the woods. The next slide was the King's Villa, or rather, a shadow of the King's Villa, the grounds of which were open to the public when the king was not in residence. I listened to my father explain that he liked his photographs of the King's Villa too much to send, so though he was describing the villa on the tape, the family would have to wait to see actual pictures of it until he came home.

The bell rang, a new slide. He rattled off descriptions of the bottles on his nightstand: sherry, dry vermouth, and scotch.

The socialist government, he said, was responsible for the exorbitant booze prices in Sweden at the time. My father bought his liquor on weekend trips to other countries. I wondered about those other countries. Where did he go? With whom?

Another bell. His friend Frederick, a Swede "who knows something about everything." Another bell. He described his bathroom, which he claimed was well designed and far more efficient than American bathrooms. That's it, there, right there; a glimpse of the architect my father would become. The showerhead, he explained, can be removed from its hook on the wall and you can "position the nozzle to use it any way you want, sounds sorta dirty, doesn't it?" I picture his parents rolling their eyes as their living room fills with their son's voice. Another bell. The way he said "picture" sounded like "pitcher." Another bell. His friend Jane, "a far-out girl who talks too fast." Another bell. His kitchen had ten drawers. Another bell. Nikola: "We were sorta hot and heavy for a while but that's sorta died down."

At the tape's end, my father was in a room with his friends. Frederick. Jane. Nikola. Hans. Carol. Others. They sang: "Merry Christmas to you, Merry Christmas to you, Merry Christmas, Louis's family, Merry Christmas to you." They clapped and cheered, and the tape cut off. I wondered what I always wondered: Where were these people now? What were their memories of him?

A voice was missing from the tape. Daniel. He had been my father's roommate at UC Berkeley. They had traveled together in Europe on my father's Christmas break from school in Stockholm. Daniel must have arrived after my father made the tape, because there is no mention of him. I suspect they were more than roommates. I suspect that he was my father's first love.

*   *   *

MY FATHER RAN away to Sweden. But first he ran away to college. He wanted to go to UC Berkeley, but his parents told him absolutely not. It was 1970. They read the newspaper. They knew about *that* Berkeley: the Free Speech Movement, the Anti-War Movement with its Vietnam Day March and Stop the Draft Week, the Hare Krishnas, the psychedelic newspapers peddled on campus for loose change, the men who never found the time to visit a barber, and the women who couldn't hold on to their bras. So my father went to UC Irvine. But he was too close to Bakersfield, and he could still feel the weight of home on his shoulders. He begged his parents to let him transfer until they were tired of listening and agreed to pay for his sophomore year at Berkeley. After that it was Stockholm for his junior year abroad. Stockholm was even more freethinking than Berkeley and even farther away. But it wasn't just that. Part of Stockholm's appeal for my father was that it was so random a choice, so unexpected. No one else he knew dreamt of Stockholm. They talked about San Francisco mostly. New York, maybe. London, maybe. But not some city in Sweden. Stockholm was all his. He would find acceptance there. He would get a reprieve from the people who didn't know him or his family's name, which was plastered all over Bakersfield thanks to his father's career in law enforcement.

In Stockholm, he could be whoever and whatever he wanted.

These are the truths I pieced together as a child who eavesdropped and a teenager who asked questions. Eavesdropping came first, of course, and it was easy. When my adults gathered, I would wait until my mom, my aunts, or my grandparents had forgotten I was there and let slip some comment. I'd stash away whatever they'd dropped with the rest of my collection. At night, in bed, I'd spread the facts out in my mind and try to make them fit together until I finally fell asleep. But they amounted to little. Most of the youths in the 1960s and '70s were looking to get away from their parents, not un-like every generation. So I came back to the tape, which was warmer and kinder than my father often was in the flesh. It was the most personal thing of his that I had.

MY GRANDMOTHER PRESENTED the tape to me the summer I was sixteen, five years after my father's death. We were standing in her driveway in Pismo Beach, California, where my grandparents had moved when they left Bakersfield. The day was clear and bright, but the sunshine was cool, the way it often is near the ocean. Up north, in the Valley, sunny days mean airless heat and sweat stains on your bicycle seat. But in Pismo it was rarely warm.

My grandmother's posture, as always, was textbook. Her hair, thick like cotton, silvery like a prize, caught the sunlight. Her eyes looked right through me, and she held something I could not identify.

"You should have this . . . I think," she said.

She handed me the tape. I believed immediately it was important. I wanted it to be important.

My grandmother turned away from me and walked up the steps to the back door. I got in the car and put the case in the glove compartment. My grandmother looked down, her hands gripping the railing. She watched me back out. I raised my arm and waved. In return, she held up her palm, unmoving. Giving me the tape, I knew, had been hard for her. Not because she wanted to keep it. I suspect she had listened to it only once, when it had arrived in the mail some twenty-eight years earlier. Hard because giving me this tape, giving me my father's voice, was the closest she and I had ever come to talking about him.

I kept the tape for months before I listened to it. I put it in a folder marked DAD'S VOICE and locked it in my filing cabinet where I kept homework assignments, summer job applications, and flyers for the improvisational troupe in which I was a founding member. The cabinet held everything that meant anything to me.

I spent weeks thinking about that tape. I thought about it while kissing boys on moonlit porches and translating Latin passages poorly. I thought about it waiting for green lights and spreading wasabi on sushi at Mikuni's. But I left it alone. I pretended not to see it when I retrieved my chemistry notes from the filing cabinet. I wanted the tape to reveal the secret of this man who meant so much to me, but of whom I knew so little. But what if it didn't? What if I was disappointed? Once I listened to it, it would be over. I'd know or still not know. I was tired of disappointment. I wasn't ready to stop hoping that the tape would illuminate my father, make me understand him and see him, finally, whole.

I wanted to ask my mother if she knew what was on the tape, but I was nervous about bringing it up with her. My mother has always told me exactly what she thinks—by her facial expressions, her words, a hand gesture, or all three. I needed to know if she thought the tape mattered. So I asked.

"It's him. Describing a bunch of pictures he took in Sweden. He sent it home with a box of slides. They were supposed to play the tape and look at the slides."

"Did they?" I asked.

"Why wouldn't they?"

I shrugged.

"Are you going to listen to it?" my mother asked.

I shrugged again.

"I knew a girl in college who never opened her law school admissions letter. She just couldn't do it."

"She never opened it?" I asked.

"Not as far as I know."

* * *

AVOIDING THE TAPE was exhausting. When I made my bed, when I listened to the radio, when I watched TV, when I stood in my closet trying to decide what to wear, when I talked on the phone, I was aware of the tape behind me locked away in the dark. I felt like it was watching me. Finally, after school, alone in my mother's house, I unlocked the cabinet.

I sat as far as possible from the stereo. My back pressed hard against the wall my mother and I had painted a deep, rich burgundy. I turned on the overhead light as well as every lamp. Then I listened. I listened to the whole thing. And somehow, by the time my father's voice said goodbye, I found myself across the room lying on my stomach next to the stereo. My ear was pressed to the hardwood floor, and I felt my father's voice in my arms, in my fingertips, in my legs, in my toes, in my heart. For forty-five minutes he had been in the room with me. We had been together, just the two of us, only this time he was healthy. Not sick. Only this time he was alive. Not dead. I could see clearly the twinkle that must have been in his eye when he recorded the tape—his eyes had always sparkled when he was being playful. There was no bitterness, none of the inappropriate indignation I had witnessed in him.

My cheeks were wet. I remained on the floor, listening to the whirl of the tape automatically rewinding, going back to the beginning. I wished I could rewind so easily. I wondered what it was like to have the type of childhood in which you believed your parents were invincible and only slowly, at your own pace, chipped away at the knowledge that they, too, were vulnerable and fallible.

2

———— ✦ ⋮ ✦ ————

WHEN I WAS EIGHT YEARS OLD MY FATHER invited me to join him on a trip around the world. It was the most sublime invitation I could ever have imagined. More than anything, I wanted my father to like me, and by asking me to travel with him he was offering proof that he did. He asked in the gentlest, most nonchalant way, as if it were obvious that he would want us to see the world together, as if it had never occurred to him that it could be any other way.

Sometimes, my father made me very happy.

We were in Sacramento having lunch in a strip mall. The restaurant was long and narrow, and the single large window at the entrance near the cash register was heavily tinted so that the afternoon light made everything look murky and brown. I was petulant because I was missing a television marathon of one of my favorite sitcoms.

"I want to take a trip around the world," he said.

I stopped slurping my noodles and peered up at him over the rim of the bowl. First I thought he was only trying to lift me out of my dour mood with fantasy. Second I thought he was leaving.

"Don't go."

He shook his head and smiled. "I want you to come with me."

I didn't believe him. "You do?"

He nodded. "Twelve months, just you and me, kiddo."

Kiddo.

"Where will we go?" I asked.

Now I was excited. I hadn't known it before this moment, but suddenly the thing I wanted more than anything was to travel around the world with my dad.

"Everywhere," he replied. "I want to go back to Stockholm. And I've never been to Southeast Asia. I'd like to see Angkor Wat."

"Anchor . . . what?"

"It's a temple. I want to see the temples in Cambodia. Where do you want to go?"

I knew exactly where I wanted to go.

"Paris."

"Then we'll go to Paris."

"Really?" My voice caught. I was afraid to believe him. I was afraid this was only a game.

"Yes, yes!" he said.

Paris, to me, at that age, was the most exotic, magical place I could imagine. I had seen pictures of the Eiffel Tower and the boulevards ablaze in white lights after dark. It had looked to me like the starry night sky pulled down to earth. I forgot about my missed television show. This was every child's dream—real life surpassing the excitement and beauty of TV. My life was about to be better than TV. A year without school. A year with my dad.

We drove home the usual way. Only it didn't look like the usual way, and it didn't feel like it, either. The edges of my life had softened, and it seemed to me that everything we passed had a Jesus halo around it. The traffic lights glowed. The man wearing the sandwich board was dancing fast. The GOING OUT OF BUSINESS sign, which had been hanging from the roof of the rug store for years, looked bright and cheery. The world was a beautiful place. I was Paris-bound.

MY PARENTS DISCUSSED the trip in my mother's kitchen. My mother stood on one side of her kitchen counter and my father stood on the other. This was my mother's dream kitchen. After my parents separated in 1990 she remodeled her house and gave herself a white kitchen with wood-paneled appliances painted white, recessed lighting, and large windows with white lace curtains. It was a feminine kitchen—bright and inviting and entirely unlike anything that my father, the architect and a Frank Lloyd Wright admirer, would ever have agreed to. It was the center of my mother's house, the warmest room in the rainy winters and the room with the most light in the summers. It had a breakfast nook ideal for doing homework, spreading out the Sunday comics, and eating the black olives I sometimes stuck on my fingertips. This was my mother's turf. She had the home field advantage, and she was ready to play.

My mother is small (just five foot three) and tucked into herself, never letting on what she's thinking until she's ready. If not for her complete disinterest in risk, she would have made an excellent poker player. People underestimate my mother, but she's a pistol, and my father knew it. Her face was stony and indecipherable that day. She didn't want me taken out of school. She didn't want to be apart from me for an entire year. My father was being selfish and impractical. What if something happened while we were abroad? Who would take care of me if he got sick?

That was the moment I realized we weren't going to Paris. I had listened and watched silently as they argued. But when my father turned to me, noticed me sitting there at the breakfast table, I knew. They went on talking, but I had seen his face.

His eyes were cloudy, and he looked weary. My mother was right, of course. Even I could see that. This grandiose plan was something my father wanted, but it wasn't something that made sense. I was angry. He had swept me up in a fantasy, after all, and I understood that not only were we not going to take this trip, but that it had never been a possibility. It had never been real. And I had fallen for it.

I stalked out of the kitchen, leaving my father there alone to lose steam and concede to my mother's prudence.

Later, he knocked on my door; he was going back to his house for the night. I was on my bed reading.

"I came to say good night," he said.

Silence.

"Victoria. Won't you say goodbye?"

He waited.

"So we're not going?" I asked, a part of me still hopeful.

"No. We aren't."

"And we're never going?"

I slammed my book shut, but it was a paperback and didn't really have the effect I was going for.

"Your mother's right," he replied.

Suddenly, I hated him. I hated him for getting my hopes up. I hated him for not fighting harder. He didn't care enough.

"I'm sorry," he said.

"I want to go to Paris," I mumbled.

"You will. Someday. With someone else."

I was eight years old. He was my father. There was no one else.

Summer came and we stayed home. Fall came and I went back to school. My father took the money he would have spent on our trip and remodeled his kitchen. That's how my family spent the early nineties. We gutted and remodeled our homes, making them shiny and new and unrecognizable. His trip to Cambodia became a kitchen island inlaid with marble and a stainless steel sink with a long, graceful faucet that looked like the neck of a swan. My trip to Paris became his cherry-wood kitchen cabinets with rippled, opaque glass that concealed rows of juice glasses, soup bowls, and cans of Ensure, which his doctor had advised him to drink. Each time I turned on the faucet or pulled back the door to one of the cupboards, I wondered what Angkor Wat looked like and what it would have felt like to take a walk in Paris with my dad.

When I realized that my father and I were not going to take our grand trip around the world, I was disappointed and sad. I was an eight-year-old who hadn't gotten what she wanted and my reaction was typical—pouty and obnoxious. But had I thought about it long enough, even at that age, I would have guessed I'd get over it. I would have assumed it would eventually become just a shrug. Just another *oh well*. But it didn't. The more time that passed, the more our abandoned trip weighed on me. In the years after my father's death, I wondered more and more what that time with him would have been like. To have been alone with my father all those weeks and months, to have seen him outside of his bed, outside of his home, to have been with him in a new context.

People are different when they travel. When they don't have the security of home, and everything is strange. When they have to place their trust in the foreign, they are forced to be more themselves—whoever that may be. Who would we have been, stripped of the familiar, relying on new languages and new currencies? Maybe the real me could have come out on that trip, and my dad would have seen her. Then what? What if he had glimpsed not just that eight-year-old girl on the banks of the Seine, but his adult daughter, too? What would he have thought? I knew the girl I had tried to be, but I wasn't sure who that adult daughter was. Or even where she was. I had to find her.

I became convinced that in the far-flung places he had

wanted to visit with me were the answers to him, to his relationship with his college roommate Daniel, to his marriage to my mother. And maybe, too, I'd find some of the answers to myself. I was twenty-three years old and full of questions. I wasn't alone in that. But I felt alone. I kept trying to connect with people, but I wasn't any good at it. This, my father and I shared, and for a long time I had been happy to share anything at all with him. But he had been dead for twelve years now, and enough was enough. I wanted to be better than him at letting people in. But I also didn't want to abandon him. If I started connecting to all these new people, would I lose my connection to my father? I didn't want to betray him, but living my life the way he had taught me wasn't working.

I used to be a sad little girl. I didn't want to be a sad woman.

I had to go to Cambodia. I had to see Angkor Wat. I had to go to Stockholm. I had to see the city and life he described on that tape, the place where he and Daniel had been together and where maybe he had been happy. I had to go to Paris. I had to see the city that had meant so much to me as a little girl, the city I had wanted to see most and first with my father. The city of light. The city of love. I needed to take the trip he and I had planned to take together. I didn't have a choice. I needed to make peace with my father as I had known him in life as well as I now knew him in death, because while he'd always be forty-four, I'd gone on accumulating birthdays. Every year, my understanding of him continued to evolve. Our relationship was still alive. I felt trapped beneath it and all of the unanswered questions he left behind. I needed to be set free. I needed to say goodbye.

But, first, there was William.

3

WE MET AT A 1950S-THEMED COCKTAIL PARTY in New York City. I had just graduated from college and moved downtown. William wore a three-piece suit, and his sandy hair was slicked back. I wore a navy dress with white polka dots and painted my lips red. We drank one Tom Collin after another and danced to Doris Day singing, appropriately, "Que Sera, Sera (Whatever Will Be, Will Be)." His watery blue eyes never left my face. He was too intense, trying too hard. When Doris stopped singing, I said I had to go. He said, still holding my dancing hand, "Isn't that the way it always happens?" He looked so sad, and the thought flashed across my mind, *This man has a broken heart.* I should have paid more attention to that thought. Instead, I smiled and said, "It was nice meeting you."

I forgot about William almost immediately. As I was leaving the party, another man caught up with me on the stairs. We had spoken earlier in the evening, and I had spent our brief conversation trying to figure out what was wrong with him. He reminded me of Barbie's Ken. Attractive in a way that made me sleepy. He was clean-cut with light brown hair and hazel eyes. He had some sort of mildly interesting quasi-foreign background involving one of the un-exotic countries in the European

Union. But then he also had family in Vermont or New Hampshire. He was a writer of some kind, so that was nice. But his name was Bernard, which was also the name of a Yorkshire terrier I knew. And he—the man, not the dog—was creepy.

Now we were on the sidewalk together. I just wanted to go home, and, as it was, I lived only a block away. But I didn't want him to know that. He suggested we get a drink. I didn't want a drink, but I was ill prepared and stupid and could think of nothing else to say besides, "Okay." We had one drink at a crowded bar on the nearest avenue. I yawned often. He insisted on walking me home, and I spent that short walk angry with myself. Angry that I couldn't just say goodbye. Angry that he would know where I lived. Angry that I was so foolish.

On my stoop, I said good night. He grabbed me and shoved his tongue down my throat, wrapping his arms around me and gripping my backside with such force that in the morning I would notice a firework of burst blood vessels on my ass cheek. He stopped kissing me but didn't let go.

"How 'bout I come up?" To which I replied, "No, I don't think so." If only I could have said that from the beginning. He smirked and said, "Next time." Then he skipped lightly to the curb, hailed a cab, and was gone.

WHEN WILLIAM ASKED me out three days later, it took a moment to remember who he was. I was hesitant, but I didn't think he was creepy, and I thought I could handle a guy with a broken heart better than a creep.

On our first date we were out until well after two in the morning despite the fact we both had to get up for work the next day. This time I liked him. He didn't try too hard the way he had at the party. He was more relaxed, and all night we didn't talk so much as dissect—we pulled and prodded at ideas and curiosities, and I forgot I was on a date. After drinks and dinner, we walked to a jazz bar. We sat at the bar drinking scotch and listening to a trumpet player standing on a window seat that doubled as a tiny stage. Between songs, William gave me a half smile and told me, "I'm so happy right now." At the end of the evening, he cupped my face in his hands and held my gaze before kissing me softly but with conviction. It was one of the best first kisses I'd ever had. After we said our good nights, I watched him cross the street. When he reached the corner, he looked back at the spot where we had just stood. His shoulders were hunched slightly forward, his hands were in the pockets of his jeans, and he smiled this huge smile to himself. He looked excited, hopeful. What I didn't know then—couldn't have known—is how rarely the William I came to know was ever full of hope.

In the beginning, we got drunk at dive bars that stocked old board games and played SORRY! against strangers and friends alike, insisting that we were one player—a team. When we won, William was relieved. And thrilled. So thrilled. Like it meant something that we played board games well together. I thought it was meaningless, but I was happy when William was happy. He invited me to join him and his friends on a house-boating trip on Lake Cumberland. While we were waiting to board our flight to Kentucky, CNN announced that Michael Jackson had been hospitalized. A man sitting across from us was reading something on his iPhone, and he told us Michael Jackson was dead. We didn't believe him. But he insisted, nodding vehemently into the bluish light of his phone. He was right.

That night, alone in the middle of Lake Cumberland, we blasted MJ out onto the water. When "Rock with You" came on, William stood in the center of the deck and began to dance. His head rolled and his long legs stepped back and forward and to the side. He didn't smile. His face was serious, intent. He slid my way and put out his hand. I took it. Our feet moved together between beer cans and folding chairs and wet beach towels. We looked at each other, the water and the light from the moon framing our freckled faces. Some friend of William's snapped a photo and cheered us on. But I remembered the others only later. For that song, it was just William, MJ, me, and all of Kentucky.

The next day, while we were drifting on water noodles in the lake, one of William's friends turned to me and said, "You're really good for him." He said it like I had won a prize. I replied with the first thing that popped into my head: "Yeah, but is he good for me?" Then I drifted away with as much dignity as I could muster while straddling a hot pink water noodle.

A year and a half later we were still dating—but sporadically. William's intensity didn't let up, and the excitement and joy he expressed on our first date was routinely threatened by his self-doubt. Often, he was cold. Almost as often, he was engaged and animated and we rallied well into the night until our eyelids began to slip and we crawled into bed, calling a tie. Each time I saw him I never knew which William I was going to get.

I had been on this roller coaster before.

MY FATHER AND I were on the phone. I was five. He was thirty-eight. I was in Sacramento. He was in Santa Cruz. We were discussing Halloween. He told me I should be Carmen Miranda. I didn't know who she was, but I said okay. My father's opinion was my opinion. He thought orange juice made from concentrate was abominable. Me, too. Never mind I couldn't taste the difference and didn't know what concentrating had to do with my breakfast juice. He thought Carol Kane was sensational, and so did I—although I didn't know Carol Kane from Carol Burnett from Carroll O'Connor.

My Carmen Miranda costume was a disaster. Her headdress of tropical fruit gave me a headache, and I wobbled precariously in my plastic high heels. By the time the Halloween parade began after the daily snack, the headdress was in the bottom of my backpack, and I told my teacher I was a gypsy. That night I sat at the kitchen table sorting my trick-or-treating loot into my pile (chocolate, caramel, gummy bears) and my mother's pile (Jolly Ranchers, fire balls, anything sour). Not that she liked any of those, but she was my mom, and she took them because I gave them to her. My father called while I was picking out the lame gummy bears (the clear ones, obviously). I told him I had fun in my costume and that everybody loved it. He was thrilled. I sucked soft milk chocolate from a caramel and did not mention the blisters on my feet or the ruby-colored scratch across my throat where the headdress had cut my skin.

I lied to my father more often than I told him the truth. I wanted him to believe I was happy. *See? Look at me! I'm your really happy, perfect little girl who loves you!* I didn't realize that I was responding to his own unhappiness, his darkness, which followed him like a shadow. He was often silent, and sometimes he didn't answer when I spoke, as if his body were there but not his mind. I didn't know where he went, but it felt as though he were trying to escape me. So, I tried to be better. I wanted to be good enough for him to stay.

I held myself together for my father and crumpled for my mother. More often than not, she dealt with my meltdowns, my back talk, and my snotty silences. I took everything out on her, because I knew, with her, I was safe. I was terrified that if I lost it in front of my father, he'd just walk away. My mother, however, would wrap me in a full-body hug and hold on tight until my arms stopped flailing and my heartbeat slowed, and I was okay again.

My friends loved my mother, too. When they called, she'd sing to them, and when she saw them, she'd often spread her arms out wide and shake her hips in some sort of jolly dance move invented just for them. She made them grasshopper pies and brownies and always had cold Cokes in the refrigerator and the good Honey Maid graham crackers (cinnamon flavored) in the cupboard. She took my Jewish friends with us when we drove out of town to chop down our Christmas tree. And when she threw on a sweatshirt straight from the dryer and didn't notice that a pair of her black lace panties was stuck to the back until my friend Melissa pointed it out, she just laughed and laughed.

My friends fell in love with my mother at my first-grade birthday party. She insisted that we invite every girl in my class (all twenty-six of them), because she didn't want anyone to feel left out. The party, which we had in my mom's front yard, was chaos. Balloons and races: potato sack, egg toss, wheelbarrow. Pin-the-tail-on-the-donkey and cake and goody bags stuffed with enough sugar to get us high for a week. But one girl climbed up onto the roof of the garage and refused to get down when my father yelled at her. "What the hell do you think you're doing? Get down here right now!" I think she would have stayed up there forever to avoid him. My mother told my dad to go inside and call the girl's parents, and she stayed beside the garage until they arrived. She talked to the girl, calming her down and making sure she didn't fall. In all the years that girl and I went to school together, we were never close, but she always said hi to my mom.

WILLIAM AND I dated sometimes. Other times we didn't. Whenever we were off, I dated other men. The men were smart and social. Most of them wore suits to corporate jobs in Midtown, and they kept their shoes shined and their shirts pressed. I was always with someone, but everyone I dated felt a little like a hotel room—clean, organized, empty, and every one the same. Nothing less. Nothing more.

On my birthday, William gave me a black-and-white snapshot, faded and splotched, of an old couple sitting on a stoop somewhere suburban and flat and bare. I thought at first that they were his grandparents. Later, William told me he just picked it up somewhere, but that, yeah, they reminded him of his Ohio relatives. The couple was sitting in folding chairs, and the woman's stockings gathered at her ankles.

On the back of the photo William wrote, "V, you will be loved greatly." He wrote it all in caps, and though it was clearly his handwriting, it reminded me of my father's. I wished when he had given it to me I'd been able to say, "My father loved me greatly." But I didn't know if that was true. People said he did, but what else could they say? "He was sort of apathetic about you"? We're so eager to attribute feelings of love to the dead, but less so to each other. Even William was offering only a prediction that someday in the future great love would find me, a fortune in a broken cookie.

For William, it was heartfelt. Or, at least, I hoped it was. I hoped he didn't understand he was also being a patronizing jerk. A clueless man would take the sting out of it.

A few months after that rainy night I listened to my father's voice, William and I were off once again. This time permanently. At the end of July we attended a wedding together. The next day, lying across his bed, discussing the weekend festivities over the hiss of the air conditioner, he told me he had a hard time visualizing our wedding. He said it like it was a crossword question he couldn't quite solve, his brow furrowed. We had never talked about marriage, and I wasn't looking for a ring, but I also wasn't interested in spinning my wheels in a monogamous relationship going nowhere. A clarification was in order; my bullshit alert was sounding. "You mean you can't imagine ever marrying me." He was silent for a moment; then he suggested we take another break.

Suddenly, I was exhausted. I was tired of trying to make

something work just because I hated failing and not because I actually wanted the relationship to succeed. It seemed to me that for two years, like stubborn toddlers, William and I had been trying to jam a square peg into a round hole. It wasn't working. The week before I had been on the phone with my mother talking about Will. I thought now of something she'd said during our conversation: "Sweetheart, it shouldn't be this hard."

She was right. Of course she was. No relationship should be this hard. No relationship this fraught should be forever. I cared about him, and I knew I would miss him, but we had been unraveling for months. Or, perhaps more accurately, we'd never been raveled. Our getting back together had only been a stepping-stone in our long, drawn-out breakup. We had to come together one more time in order to let each other go. There were so many reasons I cared about him, so many reasons we'd been drawn to each other, but there were so many more reasons we didn't work. Another temporary break would solve nothing.

It was raining. When I left Sacramento I traded a town known for its rainy winters for a city that is stormy all year round. Nobody lives in New York City for the weather. That night it quickly became more than rain. The worst storm of the summer was in full swing. Buckets of water slammed against the windows. It was the type of storm that shreds umbrellas, rendering them useless. The rain was strong and angry. William and I watched the storm from his bedroom window. We both understood we were saying goodbye. But I didn't leave that night. There was no way I was going out into that weather. The streets were empty. No people. No cars. Not even a cab. Everyone was at the mercy of the rain that night.

We got ready for bed together. We brushed our teeth side by side as we had done many times before. In the past we had made funny faces at each other in the mirror or leaned into one another, arm pressed to arm. But that night we avoided eye contact. We didn't know where to look. William got into bed first, and when I came to join him, I remembered something he had said to me more than a year before: "You know how in bed I wrap my body around yours and pull you hard against me even though I know sometimes it's uncomfortable for you? I just, well, I don't mean this sexually, but it's because I want so badly to be inside of you. I want to feel what you feel. I want us to be the same."

Our last night together was no different. I curled up on my side, and William wrapped his body around mine so that my back fit snugly against his chest and his knees were tucked in against the back of my knees, like a pair of puzzle pieces. But he was no more inside of me than he had ever been. In the morning, William left first. I wanted him to. I didn't want to get ready for our separate days—lives—together. We didn't say goodbye, but as he opened the door, his back already to me, he let slip an anguished howl that sounded almost non-human—animalistic even—and yet it was also the most raw, most completely human noise I had ever heard him make.

When he was gone, I got up quickly. I wanted to get away from his things, his smell, and his home as soon as possible. I made the bed and washed the glasses in the sink and fluffed the couch pillows, which were still smushed and wayward from the night before. I tried as hard as I could to make it look as though I'd never been there at all. Outside, the only sign of the previous night's torrential storm were the bare metal corpses of abandoned umbrellas, bent and limp, littering the gutters. An umbrella massacre.

FOUR DAYS AFTER William and I broke up, I boarded a plane to Southeast Asia, flying away from William and memories of our relationship. I had failed to reach him, this man who had been emotionally detached on some level until the very end. I had spent the last two years of my life entangled with him, and when you are twenty-four that feels like a very long time. Even when we had been on a break, when things weren't working, when William wasn't happy, we had still been connected, still on each other's minds. Still e-mailing, still texting, still seeing each other occasionally. In other words, torturing ourselves and ensuring neither of us got over the other. Real healthy shit.

Now I was scared. Because, sure, William and I were done, but what was ahead for me? I was terrified I hadn't learned my lesson. I was afraid I'd waste no time falling into the arms of another William. I didn't want to be like my dad. I didn't want to be aloof and slippery, sliding from one cold relationship to the next. I wanted to be like my mom, who fell in love with my father as if loving someone were as natural as waking up every morning. Why couldn't I be more like her? Why did trying to love someone feel like trying to breathe underwater?

I sat on the plane drinking ginger ale and sucking salt crystals off pretzel sticks, and I thought about the nights of Will. The nights when William had slept, and I had lain awake confused and frustrated and blindly determined to fix us. *I will make us work. Relationships are hard*, I told myself. *I will not give up*. I knew my twenties were for making mistakes, but I was too insecure to embrace my missteps with grace. Besides, if I could avoid a mistake, if I could get something right the first time, why wouldn't I? But all those late-night conversations with myself hadn't been quite right. They didn't add up. That was as far as I'd gotten. I could finally admit to myself that it felt wrong, but that didn't mean I was any closer to knowing what right felt like. Because the truth was, whenever William and I were on a break, I spent my time with equally unsuitable men.

There was Brian. Older. With a tight, compact body and an easy laugh. Sexy. We met for brunch every Tuesday at 11

A.M. We had a rotating list of restaurants, each of which had great lighting and a fantastic bar and charged an obscene amount for eggs. A couple of drinks, some food, and we'd hop in a cab to his place or mine. After: Laces tied. Shirts buttoned. Hair smoothed. A kiss. See you next week. I know what you're thinking, and, yes, it was just like *Tuesdays with Morrie*. Only without the life lessons or personal growth. In fact, our relationship was designed to be stunted. Brian lived with his girlfriend. They had an open relationship. I'd met her. She knew who I was, and I knew who she was. She and I had even split a Christmas cookie at a mutual friend's holiday party: two skinny women unable to commit to an entire cookie, let alone an entire man.

There was Colin, a redheaded actor. (I live in New York City. It is impossible to avoid them.) We went out once for drinks and had an entirely mediocre time, the kind of time where you're excited when the waitress comes over. I walked home under the impression we'd never go out again. But he called, and I lived by the theory that unless you think a man might kill you, you should almost always give him a second date, because you never learn anything real about anybody on a first date. On first dates, you're really only meeting someone's representative. But with Colin, I think we could have gone on a hundred dates and never gotten to know each other. Yet, each time he called, I agreed to see him. It just seemed easier, which was so incredibly stupid. Not to mention unfair to Colin, who deserved to spend time with someone who was actually enthusiastic about being there.

I was a fizzler. I rarely ended things properly. I didn't say goodbye. Instead, I took longer and longer to return calls, became less and less available. In William, I had found someone simpatico. In another relationship, we might have been forced to give. But together, we thought we were safe from vulnerability. It's as though we'd been alone in a room for two years but the whole time were blind and deaf. We knew the other was there, so close, and yet we never could find each other. We stumbled around with our arms outstretched, seemingly eager to touch the other. But we never did. Eventually, we gave up. It was too hard. We left the room. We came back out into the light. It was bright and hurt my eyes. I was so tempted to run back into the dark. Finding my father was my attempt to stay in the light, to sacrifice the short-term safety of superficial relationships for the hope of something better, someday.

4

I ARRIVED IN CAMBODIA BY BUS, WELL, MINI-van, really. I was stuffed in a brown Toyota all the way from Bangkok to the Thai-Cambodian border with nine Germans. A television and DVD player had been jimmied into a makeshift hole above the driver's seat and one of the other passengers produced a DVD of the movie *Confessions of a Dangerous Mind* dubbed in German. We watched it twice. I was lucky to get a seat by the window, and I spent the entire eight-hour ride staring out at the flatness thinking that even during the tender moments between Drew Barrymore's and Sam Rockwell's characters, the German language sounded cruel. I watched the land, which was monotonous and chalky. It went by in slow motion as if we were on a treadmill not making any progress at all. The few towns we rode through were sullen and seemed to cower. Small people with rounded shoulders and crispy skin sat at tables and on cushions, their backs to their homes, looking out at the road. They stared, unsmiling, as the van rolled by. I saw no conversations, no reading, no card games, no work, no interaction, just staring, and, occasionally, a woman stirring a meal in a large clay pot. It was the same in every town. When we reached the border and had to switch vans, children with vacant eyes and missing limbs approached us. Around their necks hung postcards of elephants, temples, and children. They wanted us to buy these idyllic snapshots. A little boy, whose hair was the color of midnight and whose tiny hands and slender arms had been blown off, puffed his chest out so that I could better see a card of laughing children splashing each other in a river. Who were these laughing children? Where were they?

The day before I had bought a bag of dried strawberries, and I gave them now to a little girl and her younger brother, who was holding on to the cuff of her sleeve. They tore into the plastic and ate the sweet fruit in fistfuls. I sat with them wondering what the rest of their day would be like. And the next day. And the day after that. I wondered when, if ever, they would taste strawberries again.

We reached Siem Reap in the middle of the night. Our driver left us on the outskirts of town and from out of the darkness came a dozen men offering rides. They had been waiting for us. I had written down the name and address of my hotel, but all of them refused to take me there—they wanted to take me to other hotels, which were paying them to reroute tourists. The Germans, who had not made any reservations, were happy to go wherever they were told and had already disappeared in a cluster of *tuk-tuks*, which, in Siem Reap, are mostly motorcycles with a padded seat and awning attached—faster, more reckless pedicabs.

The remaining men and I faced off. There were no lights on the road and the bus had left. I wanted my hotel, where I was expected. I was determined not to let these men take me somewhere I didn't want to go. They spoke harshly to me in Khmer, and the only thing that translated was their anger and the word "No." About a mile back, the bus had passed a walled luxury resort that appeared to take pride in its isolation. I shook my head a final time at the men and started walking in the direction of the resort with my bag over my shoulder.

In the lobby, I stood beside a potted plant about five times my height and begged the night clerk to let me borrow his phone. I was covered in a thin layer of dust and my hair was matted and tangled. I smelled awful. Even I could smell myself. He took pity on me and set the telephone on the cool marble counter between us. I called my much cheaper hotel; they promised to send someone to pick me up.

I waited for my ride on the steps outside the lobby and watched the ritzy come home. Tanned European women in four-inch heels and shimmery skirts swished by on the arms of men in linen. None of them noticed me crumpled in a heap at the bottom of the stairs in my cotton dress and rubber flip-flops. I couldn't help but think that my father would have wanted to stay here. To be one of the ritzy.

In my own hotel room at last, I unpacked, putting my clothes in the drawers and hanging my dresses in the closet and lining my shoes beneath them. When I was done, when everything had been put away in its place and I felt settled, the room looked empty, as clean—no, *cleaner*—than when I had arrived. My father would have approved. I lay down across the bed, not bothering to get under the covers, and succumbed to heavy sleep.

IN SEPTEMBER 1985 when I was six months old, my father accepted a position as an architect for the State of California. The job was based in San Jose, a two-hour drive from the house where we lived in Sacramento. He justified the decision on the basis that the new job paid more than his old one. That he had a family and a life in Sacramento didn't enter the equation. Nor did the fact that while the new job may have had a higher salary, its location necessitated a second home and all the additional expenses of maintaining two households.

My mother suggested we all move to San Jose or that my father make a daily commute, but he refused. He wanted the job, the second home, and the privacy this new life would afford him. My mother wanted him to be happy. So, for four years he spent the workweek living in a bachelor's condominium in Santa Cruz and commuting each morning into San Jose. He returned to Sacramento on Friday evenings to play husband and father for the weekend. This arrangement began when I was a baby, and it would end shortly before I started kindergarten. I remember little of it. It was my mother who felt the deepest sting of it and dealt with its repercussions for the both of us. She was losing her husband slowly, and she had no idea why.

It was what it was.

She had a job and a baby, each with their own loud demands. Her life was a triangle, and day after day she raced around the three points—her office, my day care center, and our home. What time she had left over, she would eat something and shower. Her life was out of focus like a lot of people's, for a lot of different reasons. We're devastatingly good at subsisting on very little, especially when we don't think we deserve any more.

On Friday, May 12, 1989, my father came home from work as usual. The evening was quiet and warm, typical of the California valley in the late spring when the weather begins to embrace the coming summer. When my father pulled into the driveway and swung his long legs out of his small company car, he was wearing a crisp charcoal suit with a white dress shirt. His tie was undone and his shirt partially unbuttoned so that his chest—smooth, lean, and copper-toned like a penny—peeked out. He wore his tie over his shoulder like a beauty-queen sash. His curls, the color of burnt caramel, caught the slipping sun as he strode to the front door.

My father didn't have much to say that weekend. My mother

asked what was wrong. He didn't want to talk about it. She, who after nearly fifteen years of marriage had grown accustomed to my father's distances, let it alone.

Sunday was Mother's Day. My father and I had gotten my mother a watch. A watch I believe she never wore. She kept it in her jewelry box, and when the battery died, she didn't notice. On Sunday morning, my mother woke up early. Her dark hair fell soft against the sides of her Katharine Hepburn cheekbones. She knew immediately that my father was already awake beside her; she sensed he had not been sleeping for a long time. My father was on his back. He was looking up at the ceiling and the crack there, which years later I would decide resembled a humpback whale. His voice was tender and soft like a ballad, and my mother held her breath as he spoke. He dropped his words on her one syllable at a time and peeled back the layers of her heart like an onion. My father said: "I'm gay and HIV positive."

My mother, small and thin, was lost inside the oversized promotional T-shirt she often wore to bed; her emerald eyes were sharp and wet with tears. I bounded down the hall from my room and burst in on my parents. In my high voice, runny and bright like a broken yolk, I shouted: "Happy Mother's Day!"

That is how she remembers it.

My father had waited all weekend. He had waited until he was only hours from slipping back into the dark upholstery of his company car and returning to his other life to tell my mother the truth. I wonder if he confided in anyone else first. I wonder if he lay in bed next to a lover and cried, asking over and over again, *What do I do?* Maybe his lover advised him, suggesting softly different ways he might tell my mother. Or maybe he simply held my father tightly, pressing his palm flat between my father's shoulder blades, comforting him with touch. I don't know. I do know he must have been terrified.

In the summer of 1989 protestors gathered in Tiananmen Square, and free elections ended Communist power in Poland. Tim Burton's record-breaking *Batman*, starring Michael Keaton, was released, and fourteen-year-old actress Drew Barrymore tried to commit suicide. The Smithsonian Institution's Corcoran Gallery canceled photographer Robert Mapplethorpe's show, and the Menendez brothers murdered their parents on August 20, using movie tickets to *Batman* as their alibi.

But those sensational headlines, which were batted around the water cooler and hashed out over happy-hour cocktails, meant nothing to my mother. The world was hurling onward, but she was paralyzed. When my father came out to her and told her he was sick, my mother was afraid that she and I might also be infected. But my father asked her not to go to our family doctor for an HIV test. So she went instead to a clinic on the other side of town adjacent to a homeless shelter. She asked my father to go with her. He said no.

I was an adult when my mother told me that, and it made me furious. He should have gone with her. He should have given her that. She should never have had to ask. When I think of that story, I want to shake my father. *What's wrong with you? How can you be so cruel? Are you entirely without heart?* I don't care that he was gay. I'm glad he married my mother—if he hadn't, I would never have been born. I try to understand that he married because he felt that he had to, because he didn't want to disappoint—or lose—his parents. He was raised in a different time in a conservative pocket of a liberal state. His parents loved him fiercely, but or maybe because they did, they were strict. I try to understand. There was a man my father looked up to, who was caught with a younger man when my dad was a boy. Sometime in the late 1950s. Sides were taken. Families stopped speaking to each other, and this man disappeared from my father's life. Decades later, a peace was forged. But my father never forgot.

My heart breaks for my dad and his mentor and all the men who couldn't forget, who carried similar stories and identical fears. I try to understand. But still. To not think at all of my mother and to refuse to support her. To be so unfeeling. How can I be proud to call such a man my father? I worry because I am part of him. I have inside of me some of that cruelty. I must. I am his daughter.

What if I, too, am truly without heart?

What if he didn't—couldn't—love me greatly, because I lacked heart?

He left the next morning to return to San Jose. My mother dropped me off at day care and then went alone to the clinic. At that time it took six weeks to get HIV test results. It was a long time to wait.

I WAS FOUR years old that summer of 1989, and I have a single, sharp memory of those weeks. Bedtime. Or rather, way past my bedtime. I was beneath the sheets in my pajamas, and my mom was sitting close so that even beneath the covers I could feel her jeans against the side of my body. She was leaning down, an arm on either side of me; I was enveloped. I asked her to make up a story, and she did, only I decided she'd gotten it wrong; the girl's dress was green, not purple. I was correcting her, and I knew I had her full attention. I stopped talking and reached up, taking her face in my hands. Neither of us said anything at all.

Most nights that summer, after a story, my mother and I read Richard Scarry's *What Do People Do All Day?*, which doesn't actually have any people in it. Just page after page of glorious anthropomorphism. We carefully read the descriptions of each profession and analyzed the accompanying drawings of dogs and pigs and foxes and bears and cats and raccoons and rabbits dressed as bankers and police officers and farmers and real estate agents and bakers and doctors. The book described not only work but also what these animals in "Busytown" bought with their hard-earned paychecks and how they spent their leisure time. In other words, it was a how-to book on being an adult in a society built on capitalism. By the time I started school I had that book completely memorized.

It never occurred to me to ask what it was my father did all day and all night when he was away from us. My mother surely thought to ask, but she didn't want to know the answer. Often, when she called him in the evenings, the phone in his Santa Cruz condo only rang and rang. She had suggested a good night phone call each night, but my father refused. He eventually agreed to a single call once a week, ten P.M. Wednesday.

Daddy, what did you do all those times you weren't with us? Escaping. Escaping into bars, into men, into cocaine. And all that escaping got him killed. Scarry left that chapter out.

MY MOTHER WAS the Deputy Secretary, Fiscal and Program, of the Youth and Adult Correctional Agency for the state of California. Every evening she picked me up from day care, and we went to the grocery store, where she let me pick out whichever frozen meal I wanted. I liked the ones that came in the turquoise carton with the penguin on the front and the frosted brownie in its own separate dessert compartment next to the corn-and-carrot medley. I sat on my mother's bed eating from these plastic dinner trays and watched episodes of *Designing Women* while she took out the trash, remembered to separate the whites from the colors in the wash, and tried not to think about whether or not we were infected with a disease that was going to slowly cripple our immune systems and eventually stop our hearts.

As a teenager, I asked my mother how she survived those

six weeks. We were sitting in the car, parked at a gas station. We sat in silence until I began to wonder if she had heard my question. Had I even asked it? But then she answered, "I didn't have a choice."

When my mother returned to the clinic, again by herself, she learned that her test results were negative, and she wept. It was the first time she had permitted herself to cry. If she was healthy, it meant that she had not passed on the virus to me during her pregnancy. Over and over again she repeated, "My baby's okay, my baby's okay."

AT FIRST, VERY little changed in our lives. My father continued to come home on Fridays. We ate at my parents' favorite Japanese restaurant and went to movies on Saturday afternoons. On Sunday nights I fell asleep to the distant drone of *Masterpiece Theatre* at the end of the hall. The only difference was that my father no longer kept his other life a secret from my mother. They didn't talk about it, but it was there, between them, sometimes like a wall and other times like a bridge, a bridge that allowed them to understand each other more deeply than before. At last, my mother knew why my father had been miserable for so many years. She now understood why he had wanted to take the San Jose job and live away from his wife and newborn child. For so long she had tried to understand what was wrong, and here, finally, was an answer that allowed her to better know her husband. My father's confession created a bridge of knowledge between the two of them where before there had been only a dam of secrets. The truth was a relief.

Once, years later, my mother offered me an explanation. She was sautéing an onion and its aroma filled the kitchen. I was sitting at the kitchen table, probably doing an algebra problem wrong. I asked her why she had not been angry. She stopped and looked up from the pan, holding the wooden spatula aloft so that olive oil and a stray onion bit slid down toward her fingers. She shrugged and replied, "It wasn't personal. I didn't have a penis."

In those early months, though, there was *one* change: my mother stopped ironing my father's shirts.

5

I DIDN'T KNOW WHERE I WAS. I WOKE UP SPRAWLED across a hotel room bed. For a moment, I was sorry I was alone. It was appropriate for me to be by myself on this search for my father, but right then, thick in that haze that isn't quite sleeping but isn't quite waking either, I was lonely. Outside, scooters motored by, and I could hear sellers hawking their wares—jewelry, grilled meat, straw hats. The curtains were closed and the small electric fan on the dresser whirled, but still the room was warm, sticky even. Another hot day. On my arm, chest, and cheek I had deep red sleep lines from lying on the rumpled bedspread. I was groggy and sweaty. The corners of my eyes were filled with sleep sludge. Maybe it was better I was alone after all.

I needed to get out of the hotel, and I wanted to do so on a bicycle. I have always loved the look of the world from atop a bicycle seat. In a car, you go too fast and the world gets smeared. When you walk, you're so close to everything it's hard to see anything at all. But on a bicycle, you're up high and you're in charge of how the metal frame and the two rubber wheels meet the ground and the air is waiting out in front of you. Your body sways and the bike sways. You learn to work in tandem with it. As a child, I was happiest on bike rides, following my father through the light Sacramento traffic under the canopy of trees, their branches intertwined above our heads.

The only bicycle available was metallic pink and came with a license plate that said I AM THE GOLDEN BANANA. I felt better immediately. I spent the day riding aimlessly. I had no agenda. Nowhere I had to be. Nothing I needed to see. I just rode—down alleyways and avenues and alongside fruit stands and between scooters and tuk-tuks. I rode by resorts and houses and apartments on cement roads and dirt ones. I followed the river for a time, and I rode by bushes and grassy squares. I stopped only once. I was thirsty and hungry and desperate for a refuge from the sun. I pulled over next to a few picnic tables beneath an awning and a folding table sagging under the weight of large pots of meat and rice. I pointed and gestured and smiled, and soon enough I was sitting in the shade eating a warm bowl of peppery carrots and onions sliced so thin they melted as soon as they hit my tongue. No carrot ever tasted so good. At the table next to mine a little girl was drinking a soda called "Foreplay." I could only imagine that someone had carbonated and bottled Rohypnol.

After lunch I rode on.

I saw and felt the devastating history of this beautiful country. Here there is watchfulness, a wariness. People appear to move more cautiously than they do elsewhere. There are memories here. Secrets. I read about these memories, but they feel like someone else's history. They are. But they also aren't. Not entirely. As an American, this Cambodia is partly my history, too. Many Americans know that in the 1970s Pol Pot murdered millions of Cambodians—starving them, executing them, exploding them. Even forcing hundreds of thousands of people to dig their own graves before burying them alive. But our American government, first under President Johnson and then under President Nixon, began bombing Cambodia in the 1960s. Our targets were the military bases North

Vietnam had established in Cambodia, but war and political goals are messy and often sloppy and behind closed doors human rights are almost always the first to be sacrificed: we killed Cambodian civilians. We bear some responsibility for Pol Pot's dictatorship and genocide.

The Cambodian government is still corrupt, and yet, despite this—or perhaps because they have known so many decades of intimate tragedy and religious suppression—many Cambodians remain practicing Buddhists. Their pain may be inescapable, but so is their faith. I saw monks all over the city, and often, when I came around a corner on my bike, I spotted them before anything else—their bright orange robes catching my eye like signposts of hope and direction.

But I was still caught up in my own drama. I had checked my e-mail before leaving the hotel and found a message from William. We hadn't had any contact since the umbrella massacre. His message was short. He hoped I had arrived safely and was having a good trip. He was thinking about me and missed me. It was one of those horrible e-mails—all three lines of it—that has been thinly veiled in kindness and concern and at first glance seems nice. But it isn't nice at all. It's not nice to e-mail the woman you just broke up with to tell her you miss her and are thinking about her. If you're going to tell your girlfriend that you can't imagine ever marrying her (never mind that not once had I expressed interest in marrying him), at least do her the courtesy of disappearing so she can get over you as quickly as possible. I reread his e-mail. What he said was that he was sad. What he meant was that he wanted me to be sad, too.

I thought about my dad and his relationship with Daniel, his old roommate. Had he ever resolved what happened—or didn't happen—between the two of them? I didn't know exactly what Daniel might have meant to my dad, but I had my suspicions. I remembered the way my father spoke of him. Not often, but with care, and almost as if his name were a safe word: Daniel. As a child, I had no idea what to make of any of it. As an adult, or at least trying to be one, I remembered my father seemed careful about Daniel. Careful in the way someone might navigate an unfamiliar and twisting sliver of a road. Like even after all those years my father still felt like he was missing something when it came to Daniel. Uneasy. Or maybe just sad. I couldn't let William become my Daniel.

Daniel didn't disappear after my parents got married. He lived in San Francisco, and they stayed in touch, at least off and on, I think. Once, my father and I went looking for him. We were in San Francisco for the day, just the two of us. I was young. Maybe six years old. We walked a long way, up and down streets. My father wasn't sure of Daniel's address. It was cold, and I was tired, but we kept looking. Up and down the San Francisco hills. Finally, my father was sure we had found Daniel's apartment. We rang the bell several times and even sat for a while on the stoop, but Daniel never came. Eventually we had to leave. We left the way we had come, only this time downhill, and as we walked I learned that going down a steep hill could be even harder than going up.

There are no hills in Siem Reap. The roads are open and wide, seemingly secretless, and easy to bike. Late in the afternoon I finally turned around and biked back toward my hotel. The entrance was down a narrow alley, and I turned sharply, cutting through the empty parking lot on the corner. I came around a cluster of hedges and suddenly there was a scooter and a car and me all coming head-to-head in the one-lane alley. I swerved and fell into the hedges, facefirst, my hands flung out in front of me. I landed in a bush, followed by the Golden Banana, which landed on top of me. I was fine, except for a cut on my reddening finger. By the time I got out from under the Golden Banana and emerged from the bushes, the scooter and car had disappeared. It was just a tumble, but I was shaken far more than I should have been. I stood on the side of the alley, and I had a choice. I could recognize how trivial the incident was, and get over it. Or, I could cry. I cried. Sobbed, actually. I was sweaty and dirty and lonely, and I was sad. I had failed with William maybe the same way my father had failed with Daniel. I had failed with my father when he was alive. Thirteen years after his death, I was afraid I had misunderstood him and was repeating his mistakes. I was still failing. And now my finger really hurt.

NO ONE IS sure why, but I can only hear out of one ear; I have no hearing in my left ear, and my right ear, thanks to years of concerts and iPods and living in a noisy city, isn't as strong as it used to be. I am used to not hearing. My hearing trouble was diagnosed shortly before I started kindergarten. Both a family friend and one of my uncles noticed that when they spoke to me, I turned my head so that my right ear faced the sound of their voices. They told my parents I needed an appointment with an audiologist.

I remember this appointment. Someone nice put me in a tiny, silent room and placed a pair of enormous headphones over my ears. I was told to push a little red button every time I heard a sound. I sat in a plastic chair, and my feet did not touch the ground. At first I swung them wildly this way and that way, but then it dawned on me that a long time had passed and I hadn't heard a sound. I held my breath and my legs and listened hard. Nothing. The headphones were heavy, and I scrunched my neck down between my shoulders. Was that a sound? No. Well, maybe. I pushed the red button wildly.

The nice someone came back into the room and removed my headphones. I was told I could stop pushing the red button. There was a second test. This new test was for my other ear, the right one. I was to do the same thing. Push the red button. But only when I heard a sound. The headphones went back on. It was quiet, and I got nervous again. What if I didn't hear anything this time, too? The impossibility of this didn't occur to me. I was worried. Then I thought I heard something. Was that something? It was so faint I wasn't sure if it was real. Like when that first raindrop hits your head, and you're not sure if it's about to rain, or if you walked under an air-conditioning unit hanging out the window of a New York City apartment building, or if you made the whole thing up.

There it was again, and this time, slightly louder. Yes, it was definitely starting to rain. I hit that little red button with conviction. I could hear! But, as it turns out, not very well. My left ear was shot, and, according to the audiologist, there wasn't much to be done. Because of the type of loss, a hearing aid likely wouldn't do much good. I might have been born with the loss. But then there was also the time I fell at preschool. I was at the top of the play structure about to go down the slide when someone bumped into the structure. It began to shake, and I lost my balance and fell. I landed on the sidewalk on the left side of my body. I got a concussion and a few bruises but nothing anyone was too concerned about. Now it was possible I had damaged my hearing in the fall.

Ultimately, it didn't matter when or how it happened. The damage was done, and it was permanent. But my parents were concerned about school. I was starting kindergarten soon. What if I couldn't hear the teacher? Or my classmates on the playground? How would I manage music hour or keep up during story time? This is when I got my first—and last—briefcase. I was given a small black case made of hard plastic. It was square with a little black plastic handle on top; it looked like the type of case that's always stuffed with money in the movies. Only much smaller. Like a child playing Criminal. Inside was a microphone attached to a clip and a headset connected to a transmitter by a long wire. The microphone was tiny and its clip even tinier. But the headset and transmitter seemed huge. I was supposed to wear them in school.

My kindergarten teacher wore the microphone clipped to her shirt. I wore the headset. Everything she said came into my ear loud. Except when the garbage truck rumbled down the alley behind our classroom and static blew through like thunder. I might have felt like a freak, only my teacher often forgot to turn off her microphone, and when she took a kid outside to reprimand him in private, I heard it. When she talked to herself in the bathroom, I heard it. When she chatted with the other teachers during recess, I heard it. I'd wave my friends over, and they'd huddle around me, listening to the grown-ups. Or sometimes, I didn't wave them over. They might ask me, "You hearing anything?" But I would shake my head, and listen to the adults, who had no idea I could hear.

I only wore the headset in school. So, at home, at the park, or playing at a friend's house, I had to develop other ways of understanding what was being said to me and around me. I learned to read lips some, but it required more than that. I had to learn to read people's entire bodies. I learned to read their shoulders and the way they moved their hands and cocked their heads. Even before a mother opened her mouth, I often knew whether she was going to tell us to come inside for dinner or ask us to keep it down. I may not have heard her, but I usually knew when the waitress was asking if I wanted a soda or ketchup for my French fries. I learned to guess: what people wanted from me, my father's moods, my mother's exhaustion. I paid more attention than my friends, because I had to.

But some things continued to elude me. Music. It was my father who finally taught me how to clap to the beat. He told me to lie down on the living room floor with my right ear pressed into the hardwood. I objected. I hated covering my right ear. I hated feeling, even momentarily, deaf. But he insisted. He put my CD player on the floor beside my head and turned on Madonna's "Thief of Hearts." Slowly, he turned the volume up. The song ran through my body: I felt it in my ear, against the side of my cheek, in my fingertips, my hipbones, the tops of my thighs, my toenails. He let the song play once through, before turning it off.

"I'm going to play it again. But this time I want you to close your eyes and listen for the very first beat."

"How will I know it's the first beat?"

"Remember how the song starts slow and then there's the shattering of glass? Right after that is the beat."

The song begins. The music is slow. Choir music slow. I hear the shattering glass, but what follows is a woman's voice: low and nasty she growls the word "bitch." This is not the beat. I open my eyes, but all I see are my father's bare feet and the long dark hairs on top of his toes. Then I hear it. The beat. He stops the music.

"Did you hear that?"

I nod, but since I'm lying on the ground I really just rub the side of my head against the floor.

"That beat is going to repeat throughout the song. You'll know it, because it will be deeper than all the others."

"Deeper?"

"It will be more present. You'll find yourself more drawn to it, like someone waving in a crowd."

He starts the song over, and we listen to it again. I hear the beat. At least I think I do. But I don't move. I'm afraid to be wrong.

When the song is over, my father stops the CD.

"Did you hear the beat?"

"I think so."

"Good. This time I want you to move in time with it. *Respond* to it, okay?"

I close my eyes. The song begins. I tense when the voice says "bitch" both because the tone is so cold and because I know what's coming next: the beat. The test. I move only my fingers, so that if I'm wrong it doesn't look entirely intentional. My father takes my hand and places it on top of his tapping foot, and we keep time together until the song is through.

He pulls me up onto my feet, and we dance side by side. My father bends his knees low so we're almost face-to-face, and we dance together but apart to Madonna. I have no idea why he chose that song, and it certainly didn't strike me as odd at the time; I didn't understand what the song was about, and other than the "bitch," I wasn't listening to the words. As a reader and a talker, it was always about the words. But not this time. Music was different. The words didn't have to matter. The music mattered. The way I felt dancing barefoot in the living room with my father had nothing at all to do with the words.

But now I wonder. He knew the song he was choosing. He knew the words. But did he get it? You can be kind without coddling, and the best defense against the inevitable cruelties of life is love.

6

IT'S SO HARD TO SAY NO. I WANT VERY MUCH to be kind. In Siem Reap I shake my head at the old women who hold their upturned straw hats in my face. I pick up my pace and firmly say "No" when the men on scooters drive slowly beside me, offering rides. I don't make eye contact when the little boys skip alongside me, reciting the capitals of all fifty states. I am steadfast in my refusal when groups of girls recite, in perfect English, "Bangles, five for four." I ask them questions, but they only repeat their mantra and when they realize I only want to chat and not buy, they scatter. Why are these children not in school? I see the same ones over and over again, at all hours of the day and night. Do they eat? Do they sleep? When?

I mostly avoid the backpackers, who leave me anxious and suffocating like thirty seconds in Penn Station. They hang out in loud bars crushed against each other, and they never stop shifting their eyes, their arms, their feet; they are always traveling even if only in place. When I need to escape the reckless energy they generate in Phsar Chas, the night market, I ride my bicycle instead to one of the tranquil resort bars where the businessmen and foreign correspondents congregate over tiny bowls of roasted nuts and brown liquor on the rocks. There is one bar in particular. It has good happy hour specials and is outdoors with a view of the river. There's a shallow pond that on most nights is so still it looks like glass. The sangria with white wine, brandy, and lemon soda is cool with a bitter bite. I curl up in a low, wide leather chaise lounge and while away the late afternoons on my laptop or with a book.

This is where I meet a banker from Sydney. I have finished my sangria and am sucking on a liquor-soaked piece of mango from the bottom of my glass when he introduces himself. "Wolfgang, but I go by Wolf," he tells me. Improbable, but I believe him. He's tall and broad with cropped hair the dull gray color of newspaper. His glasses are black and square and almost too hip. I suspect he's over fifty, but in his black T-shirt and jeans he could almost pass for forty.

The wineglass in his hand is nearly empty. He orders another chardonnay for himself and a second sangria for me. Delivering our drinks, the young waiter accidentally spills a bit of wine on the table. Wolf wipes it away with a cocktail napkin and brushes aside the man's profuse apologies. I like this. We exchange the usual pleasantries about Siem Reap and our travels. We discuss our homes. He tells me about Australia, where he has always lived. I drink my sangria and eat my fruit slowly. Soon, he is several glasses ahead of me, but he appears to be holding his wine exceptionally well.

He lifts his tan finger to my cheek and comes away with a single, crescent-shaped eyelash. He holds it close to my lips.

"Make a wish before you blow," he directs.

He watches me and, after, asks, "What did you wish?"

I shake my head and reply, "If I tell you, it won't come true."

He smiles.

I didn't wish for anything.

The sun sets, and the moon rises. For dinner, we order more

drinks. The sconces along the bar come on, bathing Wolf in a soft light the color of melted butter. He props his glasses on his forehead and looks at me but doesn't say anything.

"What?" I ask.

"You're exquisite."

I laugh. "Thank you, but I'm not so exquisite. Just twenty-four."

He laughs. "How old do you think I am?"

I aim low. "Forty-seven?"

"Close enough," he says.

"Are you staying here?" I ask.

He leaves a substantial tip, which pleases me.

We shoot up into the sky in a mirrored elevator. He takes me in his arms, and I think how nice it is to be held. I think fleetingly of William, and the way his hugs always felt like goodbyes, even in the beginning.

"You smell like heaven," Wolf says.

He pulls back and kisses the tip of my nose. If he were sober, I'd think it was a cheesy line, but he's drunk, and I'm in the mood to find it charming. It reminds me of the Gap perfumes my friends and I over-spritzed across our flat chests in middle school, the ones with names like Heaven. Rain. Cherub Breath.

Wolf kisses me on the mouth. His kiss is gentle and warm like bathwater. That's the thing about older men. They've been kissing long enough to really know how to do it.

My breath catches in my throat.

"Aw, shit, Wolf," I say softly.

He grins. It's my turn to kiss him.

At his door, he fumbles with the key. His eyes are glazed, and I see that he is far drunker than I am. When he drops the key, I pick it up and unlock the door. I get a bottle of water out of the minibar and open it for him. He sits down on the bed and begins to drink. He's still grinning. He looks young. I slip out of my sandals, and tell him I'll be right back as I shut the bathroom door. When I return Wolf is passed out across the king-size bed, fully dressed. There's water all over his pants and the bottle is empty on the floor. I crawl up onto the bed beside him and place my palm on his chest. My hand rises and falls with each of his breaths. "Wolf? Wolf?" Nothing. He's out cold.

I laugh. I am on all fours, my hair is loose and hanging in my eyes, and I cannot stop laughing. I take Wolf's glasses off and try them on. Everything is distorted; I can't make out anything. He must be nearly blind without them. I get off the bed and place his glasses on the nightstand. I throw the bottle in the wastebasket and use a bath towel to mop up as much of the water on his pants and the floor as I can. I take off his flip-flops and put them in the closet. There's a blanket on the shelf, and I drape it across his chest and tuck it beneath his chin. I'm surprised to realize I don't want to leave. I take off his watch and place it next to his glasses on the nightstand. There's nothing left to be done. I consider leaving a note with the name of my hotel, but I don't. He reminds me a little of Brian, my Tuesdays at 11 friend, which makes him both more appealing and less. I consider it a sign that Wolf has passed out. What he and I had assumed would happen, hasn't. It doesn't need to.

I walk back to my hotel. It isn't that late and the walk leaves me hot and sweaty, but alert and restless. I put on my swimsuit and a hotel robe and go up to the rooftop bar and Jacuzzi. A young couple is chatting with the bartender. A waiter I haven't seen before is sitting apart from them looking out at the city. He can't be more than twenty. Technically, the Jacuzzi has closed for the night, but the waiter doesn't hesitate to take me around to the other side of the roof and turn on the jets. I climb into the tub. It's dark and the only light comes from the floor of the Jacuzzi, fading from green to blue to white and back to green again. The waiter brings me a glass of champagne, which I had forgotten asking for. He disappears as quickly as he appeared, and I am alone. I look up at the stars, then out at the few city lights. A flash of lightning cuts across the cloudy night sky, and at first I think I must be imagining things. But it happens again. And again. No rain, no thunder, just bolts lighting up the clouds like X-rays. It's a gorgeous sight. This is my father's Cambodia: a cityscape, a rooftop Jacuzzi, shards of lightning in a navy sky, and a glass of champagne. I am playing his game, and I feel closer to him here than I ever have before. He would love this.

Earlier, I'd walked several miles in the sun to a museum, and my tired body sinks down lower into the hot, lively water. The jets are loud, and I can't hear anything else—not the city below, not the couple on the other side at the bar. The jets pound into the small of my back, and I let myself get lost in the noise and the pressure. I feel as though I'm in a machine, as if I have no control. This machine is in control, and I am happy to surrender to it.

I finish my wine and move through the water toward the ladder. The waiter appears suddenly at the side of the pool, and I wonder briefly if he's been watching me. It's too dark to make out his face or name tag.

"What's your name?" I ask him.

"I am Kamol."

"It's nice to meet you, Kamol. I'm Victoria."

I get out of the tub, and I put on my robe.

"I like your two top very."

But I don't make out what he says.

"I'm sorry?"

"I like your two top, very, very," he repeats.

He's referring to my two-piece bathing suit. I pull the robe tighter around my body.

"Oh. Right."

I have just gotten out of the shower back in my room when the phone rings. No one should be calling me.

"Hello?"

"It is Kamol."

I sit down on the bed.

"I want to see your two top more. I come down now."

"No. No. I don't want that. No."

I hang up the phone and check that I've locked the door and that the chain is secure. I wish fleetingly I were still with Wolf. But I try to be glad I'm not. I know I've been living in the *l'heure entre chien et loup* for too long. On this trip, I need to be alone. Otherwise, I'll never do better than the wolves.

SIX MONTHS AFTER my father came out to my mother, she asked him for a legal separation. My mother was Catholic. Her faith connected her not only to God but to her family. It gave her roots. She had been married in the Catholic Church, and she took her faith and her vows seriously. She didn't want to divorce. *In sickness and in health.* But she was also smart and strong. She wanted her own money. She knew she needed to protect herself and me. At least that's what she told me. I think it was more than that. I think she was tired of the secrets.

My father did not want to separate. He wanted us and his boyfriend Steve. He could bring my mom and me to family holidays, and his parents could go on believing their son was a happily married family man. The rest of the year he could live freely with Steve in Santa Cruz and on Hawaiian vacations. But my mother insisted, and my father eventually agreed to legally separate. He stopped visiting on the weekends. I swapped parents, instead.

We met on Friday nights halfway between Sacramento and Santa Cruz. I was five years old the first time we drove down Highway 99 to make the switch. I sat beside my mother in the front seat, and my legs dangled above the floor. The sun visor was flipped down, but useless; I was too short. I squinted in the glare of the setting sun, trying to make out our destination, which my mother had spotted. I saw it, but wished I hadn't. It was nothing like the sparkling secret palace I had envisioned tucked away in a rural valley of Northern California.

The Orchard Café was a cream-colored building with lifeless green trim. Flakes of paint drifted to the ground in the wind, leaving raw wood exposed. With its low, crumbling roof, the restaurant looked like it had been in a fight and lost. I stared at the shiny newness and bright lights of the gas station and mini-mart next door. My mother pulled off the highway, and we drove past a tiny patch of garden between the gravel parking lot and the walkway to the café. Someone hopeful had planted clusters of daisies and sweet peas. The vibrant whites, pinks, purples, and yellows looked out of place. They didn't belong here. Neither did we.

I searched the parking lot for my father's gray BMW convertible, but it wasn't among the minivans and Cadillac sedans. My mother and I sat together, waiting. A neon red and blue OPEN sign flashed on and off. The windows of the restaurant were tinted, and I wondered what was behind them. My mother cracked her knuckles; I flinched but said nothing. The familiar screech of burning rubber broke my concentration. My father's car spewed gravel in all directions as he entered the lot. My mother muttered something about my father and his "entrances," but she, too, was smiling. I jumped out of the car and, unexpectedly, my father swept me up into his arms. He was in a good mood. It would be a pleasant meal.

Still holding me, he asked, "Well? Do you notice anything different?"

I studied his face. Yes, something was different, but I didn't know what. He was the same and yet not. His face looked more open, but I felt silly saying that. I shook my head, embarrassed

I didn't know the answer. I had none of the uninhibitedness my kindergarten peers were known for.

"I shaved my mustache!"

I reached out and touched the smooth skin above his upper lip. His mustache was gone. I had never seen him without it. Now we looked more the same!

"I like your new face," I told him. And I did. I could see him better this way. He wasn't hiding anymore.

Inside, the restaurant was dark. A steady rhythm of quiet chatter warmed the dining room. At the counter, the largest men I had ever seen leaned back in their chair stools, balancing bellies atop belt buckles. We followed the matronly hostess through a maze of hanging fake ivy, faded watercolor paintings, and shelves loaded with tin watering cans and wooden figurines.

Retired couples smiled at us, and young, yuppie families ate hurriedly, eager to get back on the road. We fell into what would become our usual booth—in the corner beneath a window with a view of the hills. I flounced down and pressed my back into the cushioned seat. A fan above us stirred the dead air, and as I watched it spin, the last of my apprehension slipped away. When our orders arrived, I picked at my burger and swirled my French fries in a pool of ketchup. My parents spoke about their work and gossiped about friends and family. They listened to my stories about school, and my father promised to buy me a kite in Capitola. I was happy. I didn't know why it couldn't always be like this. In the years since, the way my parents sounded comes back to me. I remember pieces of their conversations, but the specifics don't mean as much as I thought they would. In my memories of them together, their voices join and I can't tell where one begins and the other ends. All I conjure is a soothing white noise.

*   *   *

MONTHS LATER, ON a starless Sunday night, my father and I sped north toward the café to meet my mother. We listened to the drone of the weather woman, her voice clipped and bored, as she reported a storm slithering our way. She predicted it would catch up with us early Monday morning, but she was wrong. The storm came on fast. Not more than an hour later, as my mother, father, and I ate bowls of soup, thunder crackled outside. I pressed my cheek against the window and stared, mesmerized by the swollen and imposing clouds spinning across the sky as they shot down raindrops like ammunition. I jumped when the hard hail pellets hit the glass. Bursts of lightning danced between the clouds. One moment a bolt of lightning struck behind the mini-mart, and the next, a bolt flashed between the rows of windmills on the hill across the highway. It was everywhere; I tried not to blink for fear that I might miss a bolt. I imagined a great, fierce creature stomping across the sky, trampling over the clouds and making the thunder, which whistled in my ears long after its departure.

The waitresses, trying to soothe the children, offered us cups of hot chocolate. I sucked on chocolate-drenched marshmallows and blocked out the cries of the other kids. For me, the storm was a production. My eyes never left the show in the sky, but my ears listened to my parents' conversation. They talked about the wicked storms they had survived when they lived in Boston. My mother told me about the time my father went to the store and absentmindedly locked her outside on the balcony of their fourth-floor apartment. While he was gone it began to snow, and my mother discovered she was trapped. He returned to find her standing at the sliding glass door freezing and furious.

My father shook his head and said, "I couldn't understand what she was doing outside. Didn't she realize it was snowing?"

I have a vision of my mother laughing and rolling her eyes first at my father, then at me, pulling me into their story.

I couldn't picture my parents living in Cambridge. I couldn't picture the young, married couple they had been, but I wanted to believe in them.

After the night of the storm, we began to linger at the café each Friday and Sunday evening. The waitresses didn't hustle. They even chewed their gum slow. The staff and patrons came to expect us, and each week when we arrived, a local tipped his baseball cap in our direction or held open the door for us. We were in horse country, and you could smell it. I loved the steamy scent of hay and earth the locals gave off. Their hands were cracked, and they had dried mud on the toes of their boots. They offered me gummy candies and mints, and I took them. In the dining room, elderly couples held hands as they dipped saltines in their tomato soup and drank their coffee black. The ladies were perfectly coiffed, their hair an unmovable force and their chests twinkling with brooches. The gentlemen placed their hats on their knees and tugged at their bow ties until they were creased and perfectly horizontal. The couples' heads were bent together as they conversed in whispers. My mother told me not to stare, but I did anyway.

When they left, they hobbled out full and wide. They intertwined their arms and pressed their bodies so tightly together it became impossible to tell where one ended and the other began. I watched from the window as the gentleman walked haltingly with his wife to the passenger side of their car. Once there, he opened the door and eased her into the shotgun seat. They looked small and fragile in their cavernous sedans. I loved those couples.

I believed that the magic of the Orchard Café, and the romance its patrons exuded, came from the hills directly beyond the mini-mart. On the tops of those hills were windmills. Often, at home, I struggled to sleep. A family friend who babysat me would sit on the edge of my bed and tell me stories of Don Quixote. When I saw the windmills spinning with ease and grace above the café, I knew they were the windmill giants Don Quixote had battled. I pictured the wiry, white-haired Don Quixote flying through the wind on his horse, swinging his lance at the menacing windmills. I saw his long, tattered cape billowing behind him. This time, he'd win.

7

————◆∙⦂∙◆————

THE MORNING AFTER THE INCIDENT WITH KA-
mol, I woke early. Too early. It was still dark outside. I
felt as though I hadn't slept at all, but I wasn't tired, either.
Still lying in bed, I checked my e-mail and found an unexpected message from Ben, a friend of William's I'd met only a
handful of times. The previous year, when William and I had
been on our first break, Ben and I ran into each other at a
party. We stood crammed together in an overcrowded, swel-
tering hallway and, ignoring everyone else, talked the whole
night. It was by far the longest conversation we had ever
had, and I was charmed by his thoughtfulness; he was full of
thought. He was genuine. Shtick-less. He was funny, but he
never tried to force a joke on me. Laughing at something he
said, I spilled a plastic cup of red wine down the front of his
white dress shirt, which is just about the worst thing you can
do to an almost-stranger at a party. I was horrified. Of course,
of course, it was a huge scarlet splotch across his chest. I should
have known right then we were in trouble. He was unfazed.
Sweetly, he claimed to like it better this way. At the time I
thought that was ridiculous and assumed he said it to be kind,
but Ben being Ben, it might have been true. The man appreci-
ates a good stain.

After the party, we started e-mailing regularly. He was working on his first book proposal and asked me to edit it. Though we never saw each other, our e-mails to one another were long and open, intimate in the way you might be with an old friend. I looked forward to seeing his name in my inbox far more than I was willing to admit. I read his e-mails as soon as I got them, and I wrote long, elaborate responses immediately. But I waited weeks to send them, keeping private my enthusiasm and growing attraction to this man. He was William's friend, not mine. Besides, though we were on a break, William and I still saw one another, and I knew we had unfinished business. I was conflicted and torn between these men and found myself wishing I had met Ben first. But I hadn't, and I had to resolve my relationship with William. I cut off contact with Ben and a month later William and I got back together.

But now, nine months later, William and I were finished, and here was Ben again. He was wishing me well on my travels and reporting to me from his own trip in Puerto Rico. He wrote that he was curious about all things Southeast Asian as he'd never been within a thousand miles, and he would check me back on the continent. *Check me back on the continent.* I hoped very much that would happen. I started a reply but didn't send it. Not yet.

Now, I was fully awake. It was time to get up. I had reserved a sunrise hot air balloon ride. There was a pamphlet in the hotel lobby that promised, for the equivalent of a few dollars, a view of the sunrise over Angkor Wat from a hot air balloon. I read the advertisement every time I waited for the elevator. My father had ridden in a balloon once, and he had told me he wished he could have done it again. I imagine he liked being above it all. Seeing so much at once but not having to engage with any of it.

In the cool darkness of new morning, the air had no\
turned stale. A tuk-tuk waited outside my hotel. The dr..\
was smoking. I could only see him in shadows and a few sharp
points—his nose, the toe of his boot, the burnt end of his
cigarette. He saw me and hopped out onto his feet. As I approached, he tossed his cigarette and put on a black helmet
that said MR. ROTH in large white letters across the back.

He drove carelessly, but the ride was smooth. It was too
dark to see even the roadside trees, but I could smell them.
I was happy to be leaving the city behind, even if only for a
couple of hours. Traveling by open-air tuk-tuk in the fresh,
early morning while most everyone else slept on felt like being
let in on a luscious secret. Surrounded by darkness, the only
thing I could make out were the white letters of MR. ROTH.
They floated ahead, guiding me deeper into the forest.

We passed a group of men sitting on the side of the road,
but I didn't see them until the tuk-tuk was almost beyond
them. They were looking right at me, as though they had been
able to see me for miles. I waved, and they shook their thermos
back at me. A female attendant in a long blue skirt stopped us
at the temple entrance. I told her I was coming to see the sunrise, and she let us through. Inside the temple woods, I heard
roosters and we passed an empty tour bus, the aisle lights illu-
minating rows of abandoned seats.

When we arrived, Mr. Roth led me to a small patio. On
the other side was the huge, yellow balloon encircled by bright
lights set low to the ground. The balloon glowed like an enormous firefly. It was already full and upright, and instead of the
basket I had expected, a circular metal walkway was attached
to it by a series of wires. A young, skinny guard sat on the
patio. I sat down beside him, but he didn't look like he wanted
to talk.

It was strange to sit outside in the dark listening to the

roosters wake up and watching daylight arrive. I had been outside in the early morning hours before, but never just to sit.
Even without distractions, the dark faded and the light rose
in what seemed to me to be a mere instant. I missed it. One
moment it was night, the next day. I grew concerned. It was
getting lighter and lighter, and I was afraid by the time I got
in the balloon the sun would already be high in the sky.

The guard explained in a mix of broken English and Khmer
that it was too cloudy, and they were waiting until the sky
cleared to take me up. By now I was getting hungry and the
excitement I had felt on the ride over was waning. I read a few
pages from a stained copy of *The Great Gatsby*, which I had
found on a bookshelf in my hotel's lobby. But I didn't really
care what Nick had to say just then. All of a sudden, the lack
of sleep hit me. I had a vague, unsettling sense that I had
dreamt of Kamol and Wolf in the night. The details were
slippery but a sense of uneasiness lingered. I thought of Ben.
I felt such affection for him. I had mentioned the Golden Banana in my last note to him, and he'd responded immediately.
"I am currently writing from a coffee spot in Puerto Rico
called the Banana Dang, so it feels a bit like there's a bright-
yellow worm-hole connecting our two vacations!" His e-mails
made me laugh. He made things seem easy and fun. Comfortable. No man had ever made me feel so at ease. But he was a
friend of William's. Their friendship would make it that much
harder for me to tell Ben how I felt. And I didn't know how
he felt. Not really.

We were supposed to go up at 5:24 A.M., but it was almost
six o'clock when the guard finally led me into the enclosed
base of the balloon. The metal walkway rocked back and forth
with my weight and the weight of the man controlling the balloon. It felt like an airborne Slip 'N Slide. I thought about the
release form I had signed on the ground, which suddenly didn't
seem like just a trivial formality. So it was with both relief

and disappointment that I greeted the realization that while this balloon would rise, it wasn't actually going to *go* anywhere.

We rose straight up into the sky until we were above the trees, but we remained tethered to the ground below by long, thin wires. It was like riding a kite. Angkor Wat came into view, and just beyond it, the searing sun peeked through a thick haze of clouds. I looked out at the forest and the river and felt all of my anxiety dissolve. Angkor Wat means "Temple City" in Khmer, and it truly is. Built in the early twelfth century, it is the largest Hindu temple complex in the world. It was still too cloudy to see a reflection of the sun on the water or the tops of the peaked temple, but it was quiet up in the sky, and seeing the temple this way, alone, made it even more beautiful. I thought about the Cambodian flag, which depicts Angkor Wat, and I understood why. If Angkor Wat were in America, we'd put its likeness everywhere—flags, official seals, license plates, T-shirts, passports, even, or maybe especially, our money. I was far away from the temple, but I felt close. I felt like I was the only one who had ever seen it. Well, except for the guy standing behind me controlling our rise and fall, but I'd take what I could get.

Mr. Roth was waiting for me when we came down. It was almost six-thirty and everything that had been dark two hours earlier was now light. On the ride back to my hotel I was startled to see the same empty tour bus and group of men sitting beside the road. In the daylight, they looked ordinary and the word "cheerless" came to mind. Mr. Roth and I weren't alone anymore. The road was crowded with other tuk-tuks and mothers on scooters with one child on their backs and another sitting between their legs. For them the temples and this lush, elusive landscape were home. They were preoccupied with the daily concerns of life and commuting, as well they should be. But the spell of the early morning darkness had been broken, and I couldn't shake my disappointment.

*   *   *

IN THE EARLY nineties, my father lived in a town house in Santa Cruz, California. No one had a room or a bed of his own at that house. My father and his boyfriend Steve—when he stayed the night—shared a mattress on the floor of the master bedroom. The room had a hardwood floor and a single, curtainless window. There was no nightstand or dresser, though there was a closet that smelled faintly of rubber and was filled with shoes made of reptile skins and suits arranged by shades of charcoal. A bare bulb was affixed to the ceiling and its glow was unexpectedly soft and tawny.

My father's minimalist Mies-van-der-Rohe-inspired aesthetic and his designer mattress, which cost more than a year's tuition at Sacred Heart, were nothing like my mother's bedroom in Sacramento. Her room was blinding, all light and no shadow, because she had accidentally purchased fluorescent bulbs and had decided to keep them until they burnt out and could be replaced. Only year after year they continued to burn, casting light onto the backs of dust bunnies cowering in the corners and across the bulky furniture that filled the room like a crowd of people who've been waiting in line too long.

I liked my father's bedroom. I liked that it was neat. I liked that I could always see out the window. My mother said that my father's floors were so clean you could eat off of them. And so, one time, when I was alone in the room, I licked a wooden floorboard and was satisfied that it tasted woodsy and medicinal. My mother was right; my father was very clean.

Steve didn't come around much when I was there; I shared the mattress with my dad. It was enormous, so much bigger than the twin I had at my mother's house in Sacramento. I slept on the edge of it, my hand hanging over the side and my fingers grazing the floor so that I would always know where the end was and the way out. I fell asleep alone, my father joining me only much later, though I never knew exactly when. He was a wild sleeper, and often, as he dreamt, he would toss and turn and an arm would swing and crash down across my chest. Pow!

On impact, I'd wake, and I'd open my eyes, reaching first for the cool, ribbed wood beneath my fingertips. Without a curtain on the window, the room was never really dark, just dim and crowded with shadows. With each intake of breath, his arm pressed harder into my tiny chest. But I never wanted to move it. I'd lie there, uncomfortable and hot beneath the comforter and the arm like cement holding me down. I'd squeeze my eyes shut tighter and tighter until white flashes of light appeared beneath my eyelids. I didn't want to let go of the moment; I didn't want to forget what it felt like to have my dad there next to me. I didn't know how, but I was trying to hold on to the feeling of the weight of his arm and the smell of sleep and sweat and the sound of his breathing. I already knew he was going to die—both of my parents had mentioned it, each in an understated way. They didn't want to alarm me.

But death is alarming. I knew vaguely that it meant I'd no longer be able to see him or touch him or smell him or hear him. Even though lying beneath his arm hurt and I couldn't return to sleep until he moved, it was good. I liked lying beside him when he was asleep and I wasn't. It was the only time I knew he would stay. He wasn't asking anything of me. I could lie there and watch him, and no one could tell me not to. Eventually, he would roll over or fling his arm in a new direction, and I'd rub my chest and take deep breaths. I'd try to stay awake, but then suddenly the sun would be up and I'd be alone again, my father already up and deep into day.

I liked my father best in Santa Cruz. He was healthy then,

and he made every day feel like vacation. I didn't have chores or homework or church on Sunday, and in the mornings, he made oatmeal that he cooked in a pot on the stove with cream and cinnamon and nutmeg and sugar and apple slivers. This is how oatmeal should be made. Nothing like the packets of instant cereal my mother tore open and heated in the micro-wave. I woke up to the smell of oatmeal and coffee. A spiral staircase separated the first and second floors, and I thought of those metal stairs like a ride; I circled slowly down, partly to draw out the ride and partly because the steps were narrow and steep and I was a little bit afraid of them. The first floor was an open floor plan, and the living room and dining room were separated only by my father's home gym. The walls and floors were wooden planks, and it was difficult to tell where a wall ended and a floor began. I thought I knew what it must be like to live inside the trunk of a tree.

I didn't enter the kitchen while my father was cooking breakfast, waiting instead for him in the living room. He moved quickly from the stove to the refrigerator and back again, fo-cused on the task at hand. I got in the way. Besides, he always seemed to sense when I was up. I sat on the floor with my back against the wall reading one of my books until the oatmeal and coffee were ready. We ate on the balcony off the living room, which overlooked the carport and a bed of ivy. You couldn't see the ocean, but you could hear it. My father wore sheepskin slippers, and he'd prop his feet on the balcony railing, and we never had anywhere to be because I was only ever there on Sat-urdays and Sundays.

"Well, kiddo, what do you want to do today?"

"The boardwalk!"

He asked me that every morning, and every morning I said the same thing. And that's where we went. On those weekend excursions, my father rarely wore a shirt, but his khaki shorts were always pressed, and his brown leather belt matched his loafers. Before we walked out the door, he added a straw fedora, which he wore at a rakish angle, and a pair of aviator sunglasses.

The train tracks curved around the corner from his house, and we followed them, walking the short distance to the boardwalk. I knew we were close when I smelled churros and the ocean. The gift shop sold neon-colored zinc oxide that was worn in stripes under the eyes, like the paint football players wear. I insisted we buy the hot pink color, and my father knelt before me, sweeping thick globs of it beneath my eyes and on the bridge of my nose. He never held my hand, but sometimes I put my fist in the pocket of his khakis and leapt to keep up with his strides. My favorite ride was the Haunted House. I knew all the scary parts, when skeletons popped out of mirrors and the end, when the cart looks like it's going to crash into a wall that then opens up at the last minute, jerking you out into the glare of the sunshine. I hid my face in my father's lap right before every terrifying moment, and he put his hand on my back. When we got out of the cart, he'd have smudges of hot pink on his khakis, and he'd only get a little mad.

Afternoons, we ate burritos on the beach. We'd sit in the sand, me between his legs, my back against his warm, bare chest. He loved the ocean. I hated the way the sand got mixed in with my beans and cheese and made my burrito bites gritty, but my father was calm at the beach. He smiled readily, and I temporarily abandoned the tension I was accustomed to holding high on my neck at the back of my head. Sitting in the sand, our toes cooled by the water each time it rushed to shore, my father wasn't alphabetizing his spice rack or wiping my fingerprints from the door of the refrigerator or straightening the living room rug fringe. He wasn't ranting about the idiot at the pharmacy who messed up his prescriptions. It was on those anxious and frequent occasions that I stood beneath him, my arms outstretched, watching his every twitch and flick, as if he were a jumper teetering on a ledge and I was the fireman who had been called to rescue him. At the ocean, though, he was present, and he protected me, and I felt the difference as soon as we slid off our shoes and traded the boardwalk planks for the soft, sinking sand. We usually stayed on the beach until the wind came up and the sun went down and it got cold and I pulled my legs up and burrowed close against him.

We were people watchers, or rather, I was a people watcher and my father was a flirt. Often, young, pretty men would walk by, and my father, who never wore a watch, asked them for the time. The time would be established, smiles and names exchanged, and then I'd say hello, pulling their attention away from each other and onto me. Once, after a man had made his departure and I was scooping wet sand into a tiny pink bucket, I felt my father's breath on my earlobe and heard his voice. "That's why you never wear a watch. It gives you a good excuse to make conversation with attractive men." I was still of the age when I read clocks by shouting out which numbers the big and little hands were pointing to so that an adult could translate it and announce, hopefully, that it was snack time. So, my father's advice was lost on me, but I tucked it away and remembered it, and even now, though my mother gave me an elegant watch when I graduated from high school and I never ask strangers, attractive or otherwise, for the time, I still rarely wear a watch. Somehow a bare wrist feels more appropriate, representative of paternal solidarity.

SOMETIMES, EVEN IN Santa Cruz, my father got angry with me. It was winter, and the streets and the ocean and the sky were all the same cloudy gray. I was six years old. We were supposed to have left his house already; we were going south, taking the highway along the coast to visit my grandparents for Christmas. We were late.

"Victoria. Shower. Now. We need to go."

"I don't have to shower."

"Get in the shower. I'm not telling you again."

"No!!!!!"

I wanted to slam a door, but there wasn't one; my father's house didn't have them. Everything was open and exposed. Instead, I balled my hands into fists and started jumping up and down.

"Showers are stupid!"

My father grabbed me hard on the arm. I didn't care. I kept jumping.

"You have to wash your hair. It's been over a week. It's *disgusting*."

"No. NO, NO, NO!!!"

The room moved up and down rapidly as I jumped. I felt my father's fingers press deeper into my skin. I shook my arm, trying to loosen his grasp. We were in the living room. I spun my head around. My father grabbed my other arm. I thrashed my legs. He pinned me down, sitting on me, so that both my arms and legs were trapped beneath him. His face was purple, and now he was shaking, tossing us both back and forth on the floor.

"STOP ACTING LIKE A CHILD!"

I narrowed my eyes and beat my fists against the floor.

"I AM A CHILD!!!"

My father let go of me all of a sudden, and I sprung up, swinging my head and body around. BAM! I smacked my eye right into the end of one of his weight-lifting barbells, which was on a rack just my height. The circular end of the handle was a perfect fit, the exact size of my eye socket.

"OWWWWW."

"See? Do you *see* what happens when you act your age?"

I raised my hand to my eye. Now, I was motionless except for my falling tears. I was alone in the room. I didn't know what had happened to my father, but then, there he was again holding a cold bottle of vodka.

"Move your hand."

I did as I was told. My father whistled.

"That's going to be a shiner. Everyone will think I beat you."

He laughed.

"It's never good to be a single man traveling with a bruised child."

He was gentle. He pressed the end of the bottle lightly against my eye. I shivered.

"You'll be okay," he said.

I sniffled.

"Is this your first black eye?"

"Uh . . . huh." I nodded.

My father removed the bottle and knelt down on his knees; we were eye to eye. He smiled at me. I didn't smile back.

"Close your eyes," he said.

I did, and he blew. I felt his hot breath on my eyelid and my lashes ruffle. I opened my eyes. We were still eye to eye.

"What was that?" I asked.

"It doesn't feel better?"

"I'm still not showering."

My father sighed.

"Yes. You. Are."

He picked me up and swung me over his shoulder. I was angry. I didn't want to shower and my eye was puffy and tender. I kept up my screaming and banged my fists on his back. But I liked it up there. I liked being up high in his arms. I liked it when he carried me a lot better than when he sat on me.

My father took me into the bathroom and plopped me down on the shower floor.

"I have clothes on."

"So do I," he responded.

He turned on the water and stood over me, holding my head in place with his knees, which were covered in wet, rough denim.

"Close your eyes."

He poured shampoo on my head and scrubbed.

"You're hurting me!"

He ignored me. Soapy foam poured into my mouth, and I spat onto his jeans.

"You're poisoning me!!!"

When he was satisfied that I was sufficiently cleansed, he slid down beside me. We sat together for a long time letting the water pelt us. Steam rose. I leaned against his arm, and he kissed the top of my clean head. We sat there until the water turned cold, and then my father turned it off and picked me up, carrying me, this time not over his shoulder but in his arms. In the bedroom, he peeled off my clothes and patted me down with a bath towel, wrapping me in it when I was dry. I clutched the ends of the towel like a cape, and he reached out with his index finger and lightly traced my eye.

"It makes you look tough."

"I *am* tough," I replied.

"You're a tough cookie."

He smiled at me, and I knew we were okay again.

Years later, when my father spent entire days in bed and I marveled at how little space his withering body occupied beneath his silky black sheets, I would think of the time when he had been strong. I could have thought about all the mornings he lifted weights while I watched cartoons or the more infrequent times when he lifted me into a hug. But I never thought of those moments. I remembered his arm pressing against my chest in sleep and, too, that day I refused to shower—his hand wrapped tightly around my upper arm, the full weight of his body atop mine when he sat on me, and, finally, how secure I had been, held aloft in his arms, when he carried me into the shower and made me clean.

8

I KNEW CAMBODIANS THOUGHT I WAS LONELY. They were right. Walking through Siem Reap, every time my eyes met a stranger's, I felt as if I were being pitied. When you walk in a city, you graze people, and people graze you. You stand beside and behind each other on corners, waiting to cross. You hear bits of conversation. You smell each other's coffee and perfume. This proximity, this being so near, nearly intimate, and yet strangers, can be extraordinarily isolating. You want to be comfortable in your own world, but other people keep intruding, not as friends or foes, just as intruders. In Siem Reap, I felt vulnerable on foot.

But pedaling atop a bicycle, I feel fast and powerful. I am not sad on a bicycle. I wanted to experience the temples of Angkor in my own world. I wanted to see them from the seat of a bicycle.

I left early in the morning before the heat became unbearable and made me change my mind. I was eager, too, to get away from my computer for a while. I had e-mailed Ben back but had yet to get a reply. I was thinking about him too much, hoping too much to hear from him again. I was thinking too much about his shaggy haircut and his long, winding sentences, which often circled back and made the same point twice. Every time I thought about him, my chest got warm, and I didn't know if that was love or a warning or both. I was scared and half convinced I was falling into another disastrous romantic entanglement. Surely I could find someone other than my ex's friend to date.

It didn't help that I also couldn't get this strange image of my father's college roommate Daniel out of my head. I met him at least once, but when and where is foggy. In my mind, he's standing beside me, and he's small—only a few inches taller than my child-self. He's wearing a red Windbreaker and khakis. He's Chinese, and his demeanor is contained, not unlike my father's. He remains inside of himself, blocked off, and yet he is entirely focused on the people around him. He is friendly without revealing anything about himself, a trick my father never mastered. He is nothing like Steve. In this image I have of him, he's slightly older-looking than my father, and where Steve was young and pretty, Daniel looks like the kindly sage who knows the answer the entire movie, but wants the hero to figure it out on his own.

I needed a distraction, and god help me if the majesty of Angkor didn't work.

The bike I rented was white, or, at least, it had been once. It had the scrapes and dents of an accident-prone life, but it was sturdy and I liked the way the long handlebars curved toward me like open arms. I rode out on the main road, and soon dense trees and monkeys sunning themselves in the dirt replaced the hotels and shop stalls. I stopped to snap a few photos of the monkeys who came close, hoping for food. Eight of them formed a circle around me. They had done this before. There was no question I was the focus of their attention, but they refused to look directly at me. I was sure it was deliberate, the way you avoid staring directly at the sun. They kept their gaze steady, looking just to the side of me, as if I had toilet paper stuck to my shoe. They were no larger than fat housecats, but those opposable thumbs were freaky. They did not beg. They were still. Silent. It was a clear, sunny morning, and I could see people not far off, but in those moments I would not have been surprised to die by monkey.

I had a couple of chocolate-chip cookies in my bag, and I got them out slowly, breaking them up and tossing chunks away from my bike and me. Several of the monkeys ran to investigate the cookies, but a few stayed just as they were—watching but not watching. I stepped backward toward my bike as one of the monkeys presented a handful of chocolate chips to the monkey who stood closest to me and on highest alert. Amazing. He had eaten around the chocolate, saving the chips for his monkey master. Still watching the monkeys, I felt for my bicycle seat behind me and quickly got on, pedaling fast. I didn't look back.

The city smells of gasoline and sweat faded, and the air turned sweet and damp. I was close. A fork in the road, and I veered left. The stone entrance to Angkor Wat rose before me. It was sweeping and imposing, yet it blended into the land and the trees as if it had always been there, as if it weren't man-made at all. I had the feeling that the temple was both above and below ground—twins, reflecting back at each other, one in front of me and the other beneath me, steadying me. I envisioned the stones with thick roots, pushing themselves deeper into the soil and coiling around one another. *As above, so below; as below, so above.* So the Hermetic axiom goes.

The entrance was still another quarter of a mile, but I pulled over and sat down on the grass. This was my father's dream. He had swept me up into it as soon as he uttered the unfamiliar words "Angkor Wat," and I tried it on eagerly like I was playing dress-up. But then I never took it off. And even though his dream was cozy against my skin, it was too big and too heavy and it dragged behind me and hung loose at my waist and wrists, shapeless. I was terrified I wouldn't under-stand my father's Angkor Wat, wouldn't see it or feel it the way he had wanted to, because I had no idea what he'd been hoping to find. If he ever told me, I forgot. I had no idea where he heard about Angkor Wat. No clue what attracted him to it. What I do remember is his excitement at the thought of being here. I wasn't used to adults being excited about things, especially not my dad, who was hard to impress. Something about Angkor Wat had impressed him, though.

Until that moment, I hadn't realized that a part of me had been hoping Angkor Wat would be a letdown. If it were not as great as everyone said it was, then it would have been all right that my father never got to see it. But here it was, exceeding my expectations with stunning power and grace. I thought about my father, the architect, who saw fields and parking lots as blank canvases just waiting for his drafting pencil. He never saw what was actually there, only what could be. When we biked by vacant lots, all dirt and weeds and fast-food wrappers, my father would describe the different ways he'd maximize the space and the views and where he'd put windows and why he'd slant one portion of the roof or another. In the years since his death, houses and office complexes have sprung up in those empty spaces, the fulfillment of some other architect's vision.

The quincunx of stone towers at the center of the temple looked bold and strong against the blue sky, and it seemed impossible that they had ever not been there. In their shadow, the spindly sugar palm trees looked like the flimsy man-made additions. My father would have loved the idea of man doing nature one better.

He had taken me once to a marble yard. He was looking for marble for the island in his kitchen. We found the one he wanted—a deep gunmetal color. Rippling through it were streaks of rock in shades of ruby and diamond. The slab, rough and jagged along its edge, was huge, several times taller and wider than I was. It had been propped up against a wall in the large, dusty yard; it was too grand for its surroundings. I pressed my palm flat against its smooth surface and was surprised to find that it was cold.

"It's beautiful," I told him.

"Yes," he replied, and smiled at me.

I felt as though I had passed a test.

"What will happen to the edges? Will you make them smooth?" I asked.

"Most people do."

"I think you should leave them like this, smooth on top and bumpy around the sides," I said.

He nodded. He listened. He designed the island in the shape of a wedge and had a hole made in one corner where the marble came to a narrow point. At his request, the workmen put a pole through the hole and attached a wrought-iron wheel to the end of it. In the center of the island he installed a removable clock that was flush with the surface; when you popped it out you discovered a hole with a hidden electrical outlet at the bottom. You plugged a toaster or other kitchen appliance into the outlet and this way the cord was inconspicuous and out of the way. My father found cords and wires unsightly; whenever possible life should look effortless. And the edges, all the way around the island, were just as rough and bumpy as they had been at the marble yard.

I WANDERED THROUGH the gopuras and galleries of Angkor Wat all morning and into the afternoon. It was cool in the shaded passageways and for long stretches of time I encountered no one else. The temple was filled with solitary stone statues of Buddha whose heads had long been lost, but my eyes swept past them. I followed the Apsaras: female spirits of the clouds and waters who appeared to be dancing right off the walls in elaborate headdresses and jewels that traced the curve of their chests and hips. They are sometimes said to be the caretakers of fallen heroes. Elegant and strong, every detail of their appearance is well considered. They take care both of themselves and others. I think of caretaking as a solitary act, but the Apsaras I saw were almost never alone, appearing in pairs and groups of three or four like sisters, like family.

I ran my finger along the letters and numbers that had been carved into blocks and pillars. I walked down and up crumbling staircases that led to nowhere. I peeked through cracks and empty windows to watch men skim enormous, flapping leaves off the surface of the pond outside. They laid them flat, one on top of the other, in the back of their carts. The leaves looked like water lilies without lotuses, and I recalled the lilies my father often kept in a tall black vase on his dining room table.

Much of the bas-relief depicting the Churning of the Ocean of Milk was closed for restoration but not all of it. I sat cross-legged on the floor looking up at the gods, called *devas*, and the demons, called *asuras*, using the serpent king to churn the ocean and release *amrita*—immortality. According to mythology, it took them a millennium, but they eventually got their immortality. They also released poison, wealth, poverty, the moon, a white elephant, a horse, and a genie tree that granted desires. In the depiction at Angkor Wat, the gods and demons are identical and work in unison. They are the same.

Everything I was seeing, I imagined my father saw, too. My eyes were his eyes. I guided him down every hallway and turned every corner, determined that he should miss nothing. I walked through "elephant gates"—entrances so big it was easy to imagine the regal animals parading through them. I looked up at ceilings covered in lotus designs and others where the sky shone through cavernous holes. Wall, roof, and floor had crumbled in places and everywhere stone was eroded and deteriorating, creating shadows and depth, ghosts, a heightened sense of two worlds almost touching.

It was strange to think about being overwhelmed out there among the trees and the ruins. But by late afternoon, I was dazed. Stranger still to think of going back to the city for a reprieve. But I did. I dropped my bike at the hotel and started walking. I wandered down narrow alleyways and ducked under low-hanging awnings. I peeked into a cocktail den with red velvet seats and amber chandeliers that evoked the country's French colonial past. But I kept going. I was headed for the heart of the city, the Siem Reap River and the Royal Garden.

Green and lush, it was the only outdoor space in the city proper where you could almost forget the heat. Cambodian children, their feet dangling shoeless and free, shouted out to one another from twisted tree branches. Young men huddled together in groups of three and four. With somber faces, they were absorbed in debate. They paid no attention to anyone or anything else. Bare-chested old men, on the other hand, sat alone and cross-legged on woven mats in the grass. They smoked and watched the world as intently as most people watch movies.

Clusters of brightly colored lights strung across the trees illuminated the river as the sun went down. The strands of light looked like beaded necklaces tangled in the sky. I sat on a bench near the water's edge and watched the motorbike traffic careen down Pokambor Avenue past the Royal Residence toward Phsar Chas, the Old Market. The traffic was unobtrusive, as if drivers were merely playing traffic. No honks. People seemed relieved when they reached a stop sign or a red light. They stopped eagerly, a little sooner than necessary. They treated yellow lights like they were already red. I liked their respect for the pause button.

* * *

I CAME BACK to Angkor every day for weeks. At first, I thought I was just being the tourist I was. I wanted to see as many of the temples as possible. That's why I was here. But it was more. I had never been anywhere so beautiful. No place had ever made me feel this good. Angkor was both familiar and unfamiliar. I had been looking at pictures for years, and, obviously, I had seen *Lara Croft: Tomb Raider*. I knew what the temples were going to look like, but I was unprepared for how they were going to make me feel when I was standing in front of them, when I could reach out and touch a stone, walk between colonettes and under lintels, and smell the sweet, moist air. It was the wet season, and all of the moats were full, the temple stones glistened with rain that was always recent, and everywhere was green. I had never seen Angkor in the dry season, but in the rainy season, it felt alive. Even on the days I didn't stop at Angkor Wat, I always turned left just past the site of my monkey incident and biked by it first. At home, in New York City, whenever I was near one of my favorite churches, I'd go out of my way to walk by—Cathedral of St. John the Divine, the Little Church Around the Corner, Plymouth Church—and I felt the same about Angkor Wat. Just riding by made a difference.

I came to love the Terrace of the Elephants in Angkor Thom. The terrace is decorated with lions and *garudas*, but it is most famous for its elephant parade. I didn't know a stone wall could be charming until I saw the Terrace of Elephants. With its curved stone trunks coming free out of the wall and the elephants' bodies in profile, walking trunk to tail, the terrace is like a child's imagination made real.

I loved entering Angkor Thom from Angkor Wat, because, from this entrance, the first temple you see is Bayon. Angkor Wat gives you room to meander and spread out.

Bayon is more compressed, intricate, and tricky. The stone-work looks like an elaborate, tightly constructed game of Jenga. The stones jut out in different sizes and lengths, and something about the resulting squiggly skyline makes the temple look like it's doing some sort of awkward jiggly Jell-O dance. You can't miss the gigantic stone faces on the towers of Bayon, which have slight, shy smiles and look like they've just smoked a massive j: stoners. But my favorite part of Bayon is closer to the ground. The bas-reliefs along the outer gallery depict both significant historical events (mostly battles and wars, no surprise) as well as the mundane chores of domestic Khmer life. There are Angkorian homes, markets, people cooking, fishermen, wrestlers, jugglers, acrobats, animals, and women taking care of children and the sick. These scenes feature repeated motifs—never just one boar but many boars and all with their own expressions, body language, and inten-tion. Walking around the gallery is like riding a wave through Khmer life. Bayon reminds me that real people are behind these astonishing temples. As much as they appear to rise out of the earth they stand on, they didn't. Architects dreamt them, and then artisans built them to last forever.

Near the end of my second week at Angkor, I visited a tiny temple I hadn't seen before but which became my favorite. Krol Ko was tucked off the road between the larger Neak Pean and Ta Som temples. A Buddhist temple, it was built in the twelfth century as a religious respite for livestock breed-ers. I had read that "Krol Ko" means cattle shed. I liked the name's directness, and the simplicity of the temple's function. It was easy to imagine men taking a break here. The first day I visited, the moat was full, the ground was soggy with rain-water, and the temple stones were a brownish green-gray camouflage. I had been traveling long enough to no longer care about the state of my clothing, and so when I entered the interior courtyard, I sat down on a large flat stone at the base of the temple. Muddy butt stains be damned. It was sunny, and I leaned back against the temple wall and let my eyes wander. Around me were depictions of the bodhisattva Lokesvara, who is said to embody the compassion of all Buddhas. Krol Ko, which is considered an insignificant temple, is ignored by most tourists, and I was happy to have Lokesvara's compassion to myself.

In the twelfth century, cattle must have grazed nearby. I tried to picture them, but instead Ben came to mind, as he did more and more frequently. He had mentioned in an e-mail how much he loved cows and hoped to have one someday. The closest I had ever been to a cow was the Harris Cattle Ranch feedlot alongside Interstate 5 in California. We drove by with the windows up, and I held my breath against the stench of ripe cow dung. But Ben had compassion for the cow. I thought about this and the cow as caretaker—provider of dairy products, tiller of fields, shitter of shit used for fuel and fertilizer.

The cow as power.

That was my last thought before I drifted off. The longer I was in Siem Reap, the more I slept. Sleep has never come easily to me, and I have always envied people who can fall asleep in cars, on trains and planes, even standing, which I can't even begin to understand. But sitting upright on a wet stone at Krol Ko I fell asleep deep and quick. Raindrops woke me. I had no idea how much time had passed. I was still alone, and it was still sunny and hot, but now it was raining. I was not disoriented. I knew exactly where I was, and I felt wholly rested and energized. Also ravenous. I wanted food. Lamb ragu. Concord grapes. Rugelach. Delicata squash. Cracklin' Oat Bran. Ricotta. Mahi-mahi fish tacos. Roast chicken. Cherry Lime Rickey. My cravings tumbled across my mind, smushed against one another and shoving, eager to be heard and satisfied. I had never been so hungry. I picked up my bike and pedaled away from Krol Ko, and just when I reached the main road, the rain stopped.

I had heard about a Frenchman named Mathieu who ran a restaurant out of his house just across the road from Angkor Wat. It took me a long time to find it, and the three different people I asked for directions had no idea what I was talking about. Eventually, tucked beyond the coffee shop and the food stalls that catered to tourists, I found his home at the end of a curved, unpaved dirt path. It was the last house. Low and wide, it reminded me a bit of the ranch houses in the suburbs of Sacramento. The roof created a veil against rain, and the house was like a dollhouse in that it was open on its fourth side and you moved seamlessly from the outdoors in. The floor was red tile and where most homes would have a living room and a bedroom or two, this home had been turned into one large dining room. In one corner, tucked behind a series of cabinets and a partition, was a bed. Behind a curtain was the kitchen and in the yard by the bathroom a large sink to wash and dry the dishes. At the back of the dining room Mathieu sat behind an outsized wooden desk. There was no one else in the room. He swept his arm out in front of him, and I took that to mean I could sit anywhere I liked. I chose a dark wood table near the front so that I could sit and look out at the moat and Angkor Wat. Every morning this man woke up to the sight of the temple. He ate every meal in front of it. Mathieu ordered for me.

"No. Not that. You like fish?"

I nodded. I would eat whatever he had.

"You have the fish. It is the best!"

He was not lying. I made butter-and-fish sandwiches with hunks of warm bread, and I ate until there was nothing left. Mathieu turned on his stereo. It was jazz, but I didn't recognize the musician or the piece. The music was loud, and I felt the bass hot in my chest like flickering candlelight. It made me feel hopeful. Maybe I would do right by my father after all.

"Who is this?" I asked my host.

"Paul Chambers. Make yourself familiar with him."

"What is the song?"

"You like it? It is the best! 'Dear Old Stockholm.'"

He raised his hands to his face and shook his palms joyfully. I wanted to tell him what that title meant to me, the coincidence, the sign. It had to mean something good. The only problem was that I don't believe in synchronicity. The idea that everything happens for a reason or that things are meant to be annoys me. Good things happen. Bad things happen. Not everything needs to be all wrapped up with a bow. Enough with the bows! Most of the time, it is what it is. Sometimes, though, maybe it is more. Maybe this was a bow moment. Only I didn't know where to start or how to express the gift of this song. So I just listened to the music.

Mathieu brought me a cup of espresso, though I hadn't ordered it. He sat down beside me. He had a cigarette jammed in his mouth, and he sat hunched forward, his arms planted firmly down on the table. He was old and gray and round and alone. And he liked to talk.

He had come to Cambodia to stay twenty years ago, in 1989, with his wife, Sophea. He had been a photographer in France, but now he was "a man of food." His wife was dead. I wondered if he had had any other customers that day or that week. I asked him why here, why Angkor Wat. He looked up and out at the temple. He answered in the form of a question: "What is better than that?"

I asked him about Paris. I told him I had never been. "You are *here*? And yet you have never been to *Paris*?" He stubbed out his cigarette on the table. He was frowning.

"You must go. A young girl like you. You must go. Why have you not been? What is wrong?"

I hesitated.

"It doesn't matter. Whatever it is, get over it." He waved his hand in my face as he spoke, as though he were sweeping away my troubles.

"Do you think you'll ever go back?" I asked.

"No. I am here. *You* go."

It was clear he was done. The matter had been settled. I looked down into my cup and was surprised to find that it had been refilled. Steam curled off the top of it, and I looked out at the temple again while I waited for it to cool. Clouds were bunching in the sky, and in a short time, I knew, it would rain. I could never predict weather at home, but I knew things here I didn't know at home.

I sipped my coffee as the first bulging raindrops hit the roof and muddied the road. Mathieu, who had been so firm and boisterous, was quiet now, and I hoped our conversation had not overexcited him. It felt to me as though we had settled into a comfortable silence. I glanced over at him. He was asleep. His mouth was open and a puddle of drool was forming in the corner of his smile. I finished my coffee. I would go to Paris. I would see what I should have seen with my father, and then I would let him go.

9

M Y FATHER WAS SICK. THAT WAS THE WORD.
Not dying. Not HIV positive. Not AIDS. When my
mother told me he was *sick*, she mumbled as if she wasn't sure
she really wanted me to hear it. So I pretended that I didn't.
But I did.

I was a kid with kid interests and kid obstinacy, so my
father and I had several arguments over and over again. One
of them was when I wanted to ride my bike around the block
by myself. My father refused.

"*Fine!* Someday I *won't* live here, and I'll ride my bike wherever I want! And I'll call you, too. I'll say, 'Guess what I just
did? I rode my bike *by myself*, and you can't do *anything* about
it.'"

He laughed at me, and I was sure I had won, but then he
knelt so that we were nose to nose.

"You remember what I told you? I'm sick."

I wanted to ride my bike.

"I'm really sick, kiddo. You aren't going to be able to call
me someday."

Silently, I willed him to laugh again. *Laugh. Laugh. Please.*

"I'm going to die—long before all of the other dads you
know. Even before you live somewhere else, *by yourself*."

I didn't ride my bike that day. I hid in my room and laid out my fancy crayons, which had been a gift from my father. Carmine, ochre, coral, heliotrope, and umber. I whispered their names, which felt dry and foreign in my mouth. The crayons rippled beneath my palm, and I squeezed my eyes shut, trying to imagine life without my dad.

First, I thought of food. He wouldn't make my lunches anymore. No more toasted whole-grain rolls stuffed with avocado and turkey and melted Havarti. No more Hansen's all-natural grapefruit soda, ripe nectarine wedges, or French chocolate biscuits. No more brown paper bags with my name written across the side in thick block letters. I thought about Marilyn Monroe. No more Marilyn Monroe movies like my favorite, *Some Like It Hot,* or my father's favorite, *Gentlemen Prefer Blondes.* No more *Roseanne,* my father's favorite sitcom. No more bicycle rides or long Sunday brunches at Food for Thought on K Street.

I thought of how sometimes I woke up in the middle of the night and didn't know where I was. Was I at my mother's or my father's? Without my father I would always be at my mother's. I would know where I was in the middle of the night. I wouldn't have a choice. There would be nothing else. That's what I imagined it would be like without him—less confusing but also just *less.*

I took a picture book my father had given me out of the closet. Carly Simon had written it, and this alone had attracted my father to it. I didn't know who Carly Simon was. I picked up the crayons in my fist and began to scrawl across the last page of the book. I pressed down hard, turning my knuckles white, and circled the page again and again until the picture was obscured and the words unreadable and all I could see was a bruised veil of carmine, ochre, coral, heliotrope, and umber—just as foreign on the page as they had been in my mouth.

He had been so excited to give the book to me. I had revered it. Not because it was my favorite book but because it was his. Now I wanted to make this gift from my father ugly. To ruin whatever he thought was so great about it with his fancy crayons. Carly whoever.

I did other bad things, too.

I lied. A lot.

I told my lies with care. I planned them on the walk home from school each afternoon with the same diligence I gave my spelling quizzes. It became a game, and I was addicted to winning, to making my lies heard and believed. I was watching the adults in my life, looking for cues and stage directions: where to stand, when to sit, what to say, how to feel. But I found little guidance. So I made up my own stories and my own rules and I read and I read and I read, mimicking what the characters did and said—because if it were in a book, it must be real, it must be true.

I made things up until even when I wasn't lying others thought I was. Often, I forgot what was true and what was untrue. In the years when my father was still mostly healthy, we took long bike rides through downtown Sacramento and along the river. In the summer, he rode bare-chested, and I pedaled behind him, watching the muscles in his back flex and the hot, dry sun fall on his tanned, freckled shoulders. I would have followed him anywhere.

One Sunday we saw my classmate and her mother. They were standing on a street corner. My classmate was wearing a pinafore and her hair was held off her face with barrettes. I wore a neon T-shirt with geckos on it, and my long hair was a nest of tangles. The girl and her mother waved to us, and I waved back. My father nodded, and we rode on. During morning prayer in school the next day, each student shared one person they were praying for and the reason that person needed our prayers. I said I was praying for my father because he was sick. The girl I'd seen the day before shook her head and announced that I was a liar. She had seen my father riding a bike and when you're sick you aren't *allowed* to ride your bike. Our teacher quieted her, but later I shoved her on the playground. She fell, landing hard on the blacktop. "He is too sick. You don't know." I stomped away, and she hollered after me that I was a liar and that liars go to hell: "Jesus isn't going to let you live with him when you die!" I spun around and shouted back, "Who *cares* about Jesus?"

My father wasn't a fan. Neither was I.

I spent the rest of recess in the weed patch behind the eighth-grade classroom, crying and wiping my snot on fistfuls of thistle and dirt. That evening I told my father I had a great day. I told him the circus had come to visit my class. I said I rode an elephant. Red velvet was draped over the animal's back, and though we were only supposed to go around the playground once, I got to go twice. My father, who was slicing zucchini into paper-thin disks, peppered me with questions, indulging my imagination:

"Were there other animals? Tigers?"

"Lots of tigers."

"What about jugglers and mimes?"

"Those, too. They tried to teach us how to juggle and to mime. I wasn't so good at the juggling, but I was the best mime."

"I bet you were."

MY FATHER WAS a far better liar than I was. He had spent the first thirty-seven years of his life lying about the man he was. Lying was both his survival and his undoing. His lies were a source of comfort, and, for a time, they allowed him to present to the world a socially acceptable image. But if he hadn't been lying to himself and to us he might not have been so reckless with his health at the height of the AIDS epidemic. He might instead have been in a committed, healthy relationship with another man and avoided the plague altogether. But, instead, he felt stuck and guilty, and he found brief respite in hard kisses from mustached men in dark bars and anal sex on stained sheets with nameless partners.

Yet, he was brutally honest with me. He had little patience for sentimentality. No one escapes life unscathed, and I think my father believed he was doing me a favor. I would be prepared for the world's wrath.

My summer days were long, and my mother enrolled me in summer school, arts and crafts classes, cooking courses, and karate and tennis lessons to fill the time. In my art class, our first project was Father's Day gifts. My classmates quickly set about making little clay plaques with their handprints, and painted paperweights. But I didn't reach for any supplies until I was sure I knew exactly what I wanted to make. My father liked practical things; he had explained to me that everything in a house must serve a purpose: "Don't have things just to have them," he told me.

Choose wisely, kiddo.

So, I made a small tray out of clay for his keys and loose change. I molded a set of free weights along the rim, because he grunted and sweated and heaved black bars above his head every morning. I painted the tray red and added clay letters spelling out D-A-D. I painted the letters a glittery gold, because although I wanted desperately to make something my father would approve of, I was still six years old, and the allure of gold glitter was hard to deny.

He kept it for three days before explaining that my gift did not match his décor. "You wouldn't be upset, would you, if I tossed it?" It felt like a challenge. No, I wouldn't be upset. I could handle it. I shrugged and watched my father casually drop my gift into the trash can beneath the kitchen sink. He saw me objectively, as though I was not his child or really a child at all.

Despite all evidence to the contrary, I did not want to accept that he was different from the other dads I knew. I was determined to believe we were safely status quo and in this way I lied to myself, too.

My art teacher was a tall, beefy woman with a round face, and she smiled too much. She looked like one of those yellow happy smiley faces; she made me uncomfortable. Her craft shop was frilly and delicate and wholly *filled* in a way that neither of my parents would ever have tolerated in their own homes. The walls were lined with cubbies, which overflowed with yarn, pipe cleaners, flowered cloth, glitter, Popsicle sticks, picture frames, knitting needles, tin cans, stencils, clay, tiny jars of paint, stickers, brushes, and piles of plain white aprons and T-shirts. It was all as alien to me as the tools in the hardware store. I had no more idea what to do with a pipe cleaner than with an alligator lopper, my mother's one and only power tool.

My teacher's enthusiasm overwhelmed me. There was a bell on the door and when it rang she would greet whoever had arrived with a grin. I never knew how to respond to such uninhibited giddiness. I couldn't make sense of it, and it made me distrust her. The more I resisted her charms, the harder she tried. She was big on smiles. All she wanted from me was that artificial beam my classmates seemed to have no trouble giving her. All I wanted was to get through class.

It didn't help that none of my art projects ever turned out well despite the excruciating effort I put into them—effort, of course, that I was careful to conceal. I didn't understand why we were gluing elbow macaroni to construction paper, but I still wanted to do it better than the rest of my classmates. Only

I never did. I wasn't one of those children who could look at a pile of disparate parts and think of some way to bring them together or reconfigure them as something new. I never had any idea what to do with these completed projects—they certainly weren't going to be displayed on either of my parents' refrigerators; my mother's was wood-paneled, and my father wouldn't have let a magnet touch his refrigerator if you put a gun to his head. I dreaded that Saturday afternoon class.

How then could I have been surprised that my father didn't want my Father's Day gift? He was right. I had not done a good job. If he needed a dish for his keys, he could find something far more appealing in a store. It was best to leave such endeavors to the people who are paid to design and craft them well. The underlying message was that there was no room in his life for amateurs.

The Saturday after my father threw away my gift, I was especially sullen in class. I was also the last child to be retrieved when the two-hour ordeal concluded, and my teacher and I were left alone for the better part of half an hour. She suggested we work on another project while we waited for my father. She said this optimistically, her arms brimming with brightly colored supplies that made me apprehensive and suspicious. "You can do an extra-special project that none of the other kids get to do! It'll be fun!" The room suddenly seemed so small and the door so far away.

She taught me how to make a paper chain out of gum wrappers. She had an entire bag full of them, and I couldn't figure out where she had gotten so many wrappers. We sat next to each other and began to fold and crease, working in silence, the chain growing down the length of the table.

"Look how long it's getting! Isn't it pretty?" she asked.

I shrugged. "What does it do?"

She looked perplexed.

"What do you mean?" she asked.

"What do I do with it?"

"You can make a necklace or a bracelet or hang it on your wall in your bedroom at home. Anything you want!" she replied.

"Oh."

What we were doing seemed like a waste of time, but I kept at it, folding with care, and ignoring her concerned glances. It seemed to me that she wanted us to bond, and I decided the best way to avoid that was to focus on my wrappers.

"You know, Victoria, if you ever need to talk, I'm here."

"Um. Okay."

Silence.

"Is everything all right? At home?"

I dragged my nail firmly along the crease of a folded wrapper.

"Yeah."

Silence.

"You're doing such a good job," she said.

"Thanks."

"That's your dad who brings you and picks you up, right?"

I nodded.

"Do you spend a lot of time with him?"

I shrugged.

Silence.

"Is anyone hurting you?"

I looked up at her then.

"What?"

"Does your dad ever . . . hit you?"

I didn't hear her. "Does he, what?"

"Hit you."

He had spanked me a couple of times, but I knew that wasn't what she meant.

"No. No." I shook my head.

"You have so many bruises," she said quietly.

"I have banana legs. That's what my mom calls them."

She persisted. "You seem afraid of him."

I shook my head again. "He's not bad."

"That's good," she replied. She patted my arm. "But you can always talk to me."

Then, as if on cue, the bell on the back of the door rang and my father was there inside the shop with us, his straw fedora and aviators making it impossible to see his eyes. I was up and out of my chair and beside him by the time my teacher stood, startled, and dropped part of our paper chain on the floor. I grabbed ahold of his arm, and he looked down at me, but all I saw was my own reflection in his sunglasses. I wanted to show her we were okay. I wasn't afraid.

I was silent walking home, and my father asked me what was wrong.

"She thinks you hit me."

"Did you tell her I don't?"

"Yeah." I looked up at him and nodded.

"Good."

I didn't understand why he wasn't more upset. *I* was upset. It was the part about fear that bothered me the most. My teacher thought I was afraid of my father, and she wasn't wrong. No one had ever noticed before, or at least, no one had ever said it out loud to me. It was never that I thought he was going to hit me. He scared me, because I never knew what was going to make him happy and what was going to irritate him. I wasn't very good at anticipating what he wanted me to do or say. Now I suspect he didn't know what he wanted from me, either. Or from anyone else. He only knew what he didn't want. And what he didn't want made up a long, ever-growing list of intimidating things and behaviors and people, and it was impossible to keep up with them all. I wished I had a manual on my dad, something I could study and memorize. I just wanted the answers. I was tired of failing.

10

I LEFT CAMBODIA AND RETURNED TO NEW YORK because I had depleted my savings and the fall semester was about to begin. I had graduate school and freelance writing deadlines to return to. I left, too, because I had done in Cambodia what I needed to do; I had seen and felt and touched and breathed Angkor Wat. I had biked around the temple. I had eaten in its shadow. I had sat on its cool stone and dipped my toes in its languid, unmoving ponds. I had returned day after day to read and nap and gaze in its courtyards and hallways and staircases and against the trees that watched the temple rise in the twelfth century. It had taken me almost twenty years and required traveling twenty thousand miles, but I gave my father Angkor, and Angkor gave me back a part of him. I might never have seen this magnificent place if not for him. Or, if I had, I wouldn't have known that it was something he and I could share. I still didn't know why he'd wanted to go, but he must have been moved by the idea of it or a photo he had seen. I knew it meant something to him. It didn't even matter anymore what that something might have been. Just that it mattered. It mattered first to him, and then to me, and now to us.

But it was time to come home. Before I could take my

father to Stockholm and to Paris, I had to attend to my own life, which still felt stalled. I had a second year of graduate school, but then what? School felt a bit like hiding out, never quite real. I knew I wanted to be a writer, but I didn't know exactly what that might mean. Would it look like all those coffee-shop shoulders hunched over laptops on the Internet reading everyone else's writing but doing very little of their own? Would it mean waitressing or shopgirling to make up for all the paychecks writing never brings? Almost certainly. Maybe some actual writing, too, which I hadn't been doing very much of.

Big shocker, those weren't my only fears. I was afraid, too, that I wasn't capable of giving people what they wanted. Professors. Editors. Agents. Family. Friends. Men. That I wasn't good enough. That, in the case of men, I couldn't open my heart wide enough. That if I could have, William might have been able to do the same. But we failed each other, and now, Ben. He made me not quite hopeful but curious—full of maybes and tentatively pleasant what-ifs.

Back in New York, I resumed classes and work, and my life fell into its old familiar pattern. William and I were no longer having dinner at tiny chic bistros or sitting close in dark theaters, but I was casually dating two new actors and still had my sweet Tuesday mornings with Brian. Ben and I were also e-mailing more and more, but we hadn't seen each other. I had no idea if my feelings for him would translate from the computer screen to reality. And there was still William to consider. William who had e-mailed me when I got home just to say he couldn't see or talk to me. I wanted to see Ben, to find out if seeing him in person would feel the same as seeing his name in my inbox. I hoped both that it would and that it wouldn't; none of us needed or deserved the complication of me and Ben falling for each other. I also had no idea how he felt—only that he continued to write long, insightful e-mails that made me feel better about the universe.

I wrote him and suggested that since I had helped him with his book proposal, he should help me buy a bike. I didn't need any help buying a bike. But he didn't need to know that. He replied with gusto:

> I am eager to help with any biking-related purchases you need to make. 1) Bike itself. I will always steer you cheaper, cheaper, and cheaper. Just my philosophy on these types of things in the city; not to mention that I will bet any amount of money that anytime you go on a weekend trip with a friend and his/her $3000 bike you'll still manage to ride right next to him/her the whole time. Gear is a WHOLE different issue, however. (Nothing would make me happier than outfitting you in some deeply sleek rain-pants that will keep you warm, dry, and fly all winter long.) 2) Your dream is real. You can can can ride year-round. In fact the winter is the most fun time to ride of all. You feel like a warrior and you don't arrive to all your meetings well dressed and sweaty.

We met at a bike shop of his choosing on a brisk day in October, one week before Halloween. He was late. I was not. I wore a T-shirt dress, a trench coat, and motorcycle boots. It was chilly out, and only later would I realize that with my trench tied tightly around my waist, I looked like a flasher. Ben didn't seem to mind. When he arrived, harried, he was wearing a neon yellow bike jacket and his dark curls fanned out from beneath his helmet. I took one look at him—Sold.

What struck me then, when he walked into that bike shop on Second Avenue, was not only his handsomeness but also his lopsidedness. He was perpetually leaning slightly to one side as if on a roller coaster, and in conversation, whether he was listening intently or thinking about something else entirely, he cocked his head in concentration. Even his smile was crooked, haphazard. His teeth were straight but gappy, and he smiled with his mouth open. There was nothing neat or proper about Ben's appearance. He excelled at dishevelment. But I was immediately drawn to his absentminded professor quality. It was so different from William's polished crispness. So much warmer than any of the men I usually dated.

I let Ben show me bikes at three different shops, but we didn't really see any of them. We were too busy examining each other. By three o'clock, we decided we needed beer. We sat on bar stools in an empty sunlit bar across the street from Tompkins Square Park. I bragged about my sense of smell. He bragged about biking from New York to San Francisco in thirty days. *It was the hardest thing I've ever done, but it was incredible.* Ben did things other people only talked about doing. For six years he had taught transfer-school students between the ages of seventeen and twenty-one; he helped start a school in Bushwick; he won a fellowship to start an urban garden. When he eventually quit teaching, it was to be a writer. Unlike most of us, he wasn't afraid to try. He wasn't afraid to fail. A year later he had a book deal.

We ordered another round. And another. And then another. We talked about Halloween. I told him I was dressing up with a couple of friends as Alvin and the Chipmunks. *Let me guess. You're Alvin.* I was. His hand was on the bar. So was mine. It seemed to me that they kept getting closer and closer to one another. He had spun the bar stool around and was sitting so that he faced me, his arms and legs relaxed and casually spread. It was as if he couldn't help but be open.

I went to the restroom and stood in front of the dirty mirror in the cramped, graffiti-covered closet turned bathroom and gave myself a tipsy pep talk. *Just tell him. This is not rocket science. You're paying him a compliment. Everyone likes to hear nice things about themselves. Get this over with, woman. If you don't say anything now, you're going to be annoyed with yourself later. At the worst he rejects you, at which point, you'll be glad you're already drunk. Also? Rejection? Get over yourself. Not the biggest deal. Worse things have certainly befallen people.*

I hadn't even sat down again before I started spewing words. "Look, I'm just going to say this. I know you're William's friend, and I don't want to disrespect that. And you probably hear this all the time, but I have such a crush on you. I have no idea how you feel, and it's not like I expect you to feel the same. I just figured it's always nice to give someone a compliment, you know? So, for what it's worth, you're amazing."

At which point, I threw up a little in my mouth.

Ben grabbed my hand and pulled me to him and kissed me. If not for the vomit I'd just swallowed, I might have mistaken myself for a split second as the heroine in a romantic comedy. I even had the thought that his hazel-blue eyes, with their yellow irises and black pupils, looked like sunflowers in the sky. Gross.

Ben pulled away.

"I've thought about kissing you so many times. But now it feels wrong. You're William's."

I shook my head.

"I don't belong to William. I don't belong to anyone."

I paused.

"But, yeah, I'm his ex. I get it."

I had to go. Somehow it was eight o'clock, and I was an hour late meeting friends. Ben hailed me a cab. He kissed me again. I told him we'd figure it out. But he didn't look convinced. He looked distraught, and I felt that I had placed the pressure of the world on his shoulders. I had taken all of our feelings for each other and given them a voice, made them real. Ben had been content to write e-mails and think of me and us in a very distant, very safe, future fantasy. All the while never jeopardizing his friendship with William. I was the one breathing life into our feelings, forcing them into something that could grow. But maybe I had made a mistake.

MY FATHER HAD a friend named Karen who lived in Capitola, a sleepy beach town less than a mile down the road from his home in Santa Cruz. Capitola was tiny. Its few businesses—an Italian restaurant specializing in clams, a kite shop, a diner, an ice-cream shop, a convenience store—were either on the beach or across the street so that you could eat clams in red sauce with your feet in the sand or buy a dream catcher with the smell of salt water in your nostrils.

I saw more of Karen than I did of my father's other friends because she was single and had twin daughters only a year older than me. It was easy to bring me along; I had playmates. Karen's house was on a hill. The bedrooms were on the ground floor while the kitchen, dining area, and living room were on the second floor with an impressive view of the Pacific Ocean. I remember standing on the stairs looking up to the second floor. My father was sitting on the couch. He was in profile, talking to Karen, who I couldn't see. Behind him was what looked like gray sky but was actually ocean. It only looked like the sea when the waves came. Up, up, up, and crash. My father was animated. His hands were flying. He was telling a story. Karen said something I didn't make out. My father laughed. He threw his head back and laughed and laughed. I liked Karen.

I looked for her when I got back from Cambodia. When I found her, I learned she no longer lived in California, which made me sad. I called her from Connecticut where I was visiting a friend. I sat on the bed in the guest room, and the whole time Karen and I talked I kept picturing her in her old living room sitting on the couch with the gray water behind her. I knew she wasn't there, but that's how I saw her.

Her voice was exactly as I remembered it—thick as honey and a slight raspy bite at the end of syllables. She told me what a good friend my dad had been. That he was always up for adventure. This was important to Karen. Her own mother had been afraid of trying new things, and whether she meant to or not, she had discouraged adventure. Karen didn't want that for her daughters. My father's willingness to do things encouraged her and gave her daughters experiences like skiing and Disneyland and vacations to Washington, D.C., that they might not otherwise have had. My father had opened her life.

"Louis had joy."

But then things changed. She didn't know why at the time, but in 1989 my father started to change.

"He . . . I don't know the right word. But he became unsettled. Unfocused. He was distracted."

Lost.

Eventually, he told Karen about his sexuality and that he was HIV positive.

"I don't remember a lot of that conversation, but I do remember very clearly that what saddened him was that he wouldn't see you grow up."

It was nice to hear this said out loud by someone other than my mom.

After my father told Karen he was sick, he began to mention Steve. But he never introduced them. "He couldn't share with people, sometimes. There was this instinct he never shook."

On occasion, though, my father wanted to talk about Steve.

"Their relationship was volatile. It caused your dad a lot of pain."

I nodded.

We were on the phone. She couldn't see me, of course.

I nodded anyway.

I didn't want to repeat my father's mistakes. I didn't want to get hurt or to cause hurt. But I didn't say any of this out loud. Instead, I let Karen keep going. She didn't really want to talk about Steve. She never even met him. She moved on and brought up our trip to Washington, D.C. Steve and my father would have been dating by then, but it was just my dad, Karen, her twins, and me on that trip.

"Do you remember at dinner pretending I was your mom?"

I did.

"The waitress assumed we were a family."

"She thought we were triplets," I said.

"Yes, that's right."

"I loved that."

"You did! You wanted to make a game out of it. Pretend we really were a family. My girls went along with it for a bit, but you kept it up even after we left the restaurant. All night."

11

BY 1993 IT HAD BECOME IMPOSSIBLE TO IGNORE my father's decline. His life and ours were changing. He had left his job in San Jose, sold his place in Santa Cruz, and bought a house four blocks from my mother's in Sacramento. He'd moved away when I was six months old, and when he moved back, I was seven. I have no memory of those first months when we were a family like any other—with secrets and distance in our hearts but together all the same. And when he came home, six and a half years later, it never occurred to me to ask why. I would have been more likely to ask why it took so long. But I didn't ask that, either. Years later, long after my father had died, I did ask my mother why he came back to Sacramento. She told me he came because he wanted to be near me for whatever time he had left. My father had no love for Sacramento. I don't believe he ever thought of it as his home. But he chose to die there, because I was there. I think that's the nicest thing my father ever did for me.

My mother was glad he came back. We were a family and, in my mother's mind, nothing could change that. Even Steve, my father's boyfriend. Because when my father came, he came with Steve. But that didn't faze my mom. She wanted my father to be happy. She wanted us to be together. If that meant

Steve tagged along, so be it. I used to think that because my mother was the youngest of four girls, she was used to accommodating other people. I still think that. But that explanation doesn't do justice to my parents' extraordinary relationship. They loved each other. More significantly, I think they understood each other, and that, for two people who had so often been misunderstood by their families, was the real lynchpin. I have friends who grew up in the shadow of their parents' ugly marriages and divorces. As kids, their parents were the two most important people in their lives, and they had to watch the breakdown of their parents' relationship in graphic and brutal detail. They bear the scars of those years. And while my heart breaks for the children my friends used to be and the adult consequences of that experience, I cannot relate. Whatever battles my parents had to fight against each other were long over by the time I would have been old enough to internalize them.

When they met, my father was twenty-three, and my mother was twenty-five. She'd been dating someone else off and on for a few years—someone with a talent for disappointing her. They were on yet another break when my mother agreed to go rafting with her friend Larry and his friend Louis. Larry liked my mom, but he made a fatal error when he chose my tall and dashing long-haired father as wingman.

My parents were only a few dates deep into a relationship when my mom's ex-boyfriend called. He wanted to talk. He sat in her living room, and said he wanted to get back together. My mom turned him down. She was dating someone new now. A few weeks later my parents got engaged. No ring. My mom didn't want one. She only wanted my dad. And unlike her last relationship, this one moved fast. So fast that when my mother told her parents she was engaged their first question was "To whom?"

My father, meanwhile, wrote his parents a chatty letter

and added the postscript, "P.S. I'm getting married." After his parents determined that he wasn't kidding, they were relieved. He was getting married. He was going to spend his life with a woman.

A decade later my parents were walking downtown on N Street. My father made my mother laugh, and ahead of them a man turned around. It was my mother's ex-boyfriend. The one who had wanted to get back together. "I'd recognize that laugh anywhere," he said. He may have known the sound of her laughter, but it was my father who made her laugh.

My parents were married for ten years before I was born. That decade was not the easiest for either of them. My mother told me once that she has a distinct memory of being pregnant with me and knowing that she might end up a single parent. "I remember thinking that if my marriage fell apart and I was left alone to raise my baby, I could do it. We'd be okay." My mother knew, and she was prepared. So when she finally learned that my father was gay and that he was sick, they were able to let go of a marriage that wasn't working and just be close. They made peace with each other, and they became wonderful friends. That's what I remember. Not ugliness. Not hate. Just two people who really enjoyed each other.

Nobody could make my father laugh like my mother. I remember very clearly being at a family party; my father was on one side of the room and I was on the other. My mother entered and although my father's back was to her, he immediately seemed to sense her presence. He turned and smiled at her. My mother stuck out her tongue at him, and he laughed and laughed, much to the confusion of whomever he had been talking to. I watched. I remember, too, some other time, being in the car with both my parents—I have no idea where we were going—and listening to my mother tell my father a story. The specifics have long faded, but I remember being in the backseat and sensing that my parents had forgotten I was there. They were in their own world. When they spoke, there were smiles in their voices meant only for each other, and I leaned back in my seat and thought, *When I grow up, I want someone I can be like this with.* Our own little world. Population 2.

LIFE WITH MY father in Sacramento was fraught. I saw him most days in the hours between school and bed. I often caught him grimacing when he looked out the window or at all the people in line ahead of him at the bank. Years later, after I had moved to New York City and frequently found myself behind a slow walker on the sidewalk, I would recognize that look in myself and finally understand the thought behind it: inappropriate indignation. The belief that whatever inconvenience has presented itself is a personal insult. *How dare the world pull this shit after everything I've been through.* Of course, life doesn't work that way. Just because you're HIV positive or your father dies doesn't mean you get to skip the line and avoid having any of your perfectly combed feathers ruffled. But I don't think my father ever really understood that. Everything was personal. Every battle needed to be fought. I don't know if it was being gay or sick or just the way he was, but the father I knew didn't have much perspective. And although I tried to pick my battles and not get caught up in my own inappropriate indignation, I, too, sometimes misplaced my perspective.

My father's displeasure with minor life situations was always evident, but his sickness was not. He was still strong. We rode bicycles, went to movies, ate loose scrambled eggs with peppers and onions in bistros with pretty waitresses, played Scrabble, and read the newspaper together on Sunday mornings.

For a time, my lives with each of my parents wove in and

out of each other with relative peace. My father was healthy more weeks than not, and he built a life for himself in Sacramento with Steve and a select handful of friends. Sometimes, I would be with one parent and we would run into the other. More often than not, I spotted my other parent before they saw each other.

My mother and I ran into my father at the grocery store. Our carts collided where the meat counter and the freezer aisle met. It was late on a weeknight. My mother was tired and agitated. My father's attitude was more laissez-faire, on account of being on disability but mostly still able. My father was pushing his cart and my mother hers. I stood in the middle and surveyed the contents of each basket. My father's looked like it came from a roadside market in the French countryside: long carrots with their greens still intact as though he had pulled them from the ground himself, eggplant, apples, bananas, red and green peppers, a baguette, a couple of blocks of smelly cheese, Carr's Table Water Crackers, Fig Newtons, Hansen's Natural Grapefruit Soda, Pellegrino. Only a cashmere throw and a wicker basket short of a picnic. My mother's looked like what it was, the cart of a hardworking single mother: Fruit Loops, a bag of baby carrots, a head of iceberg lettuce, Kraft Zesty Italian Dressing, a twelve-pack of Coca-Cola, Twinkies, butter, the red Sun-Maid bag of raisin cinnamon swirl bread, and Campbell's chicken soup with stars.

My father followed my gaze and chuckled and that was all. My mother laughed with him. She didn't care if he judged her cart. She didn't have time to care. And then we parted. Anyone watching would have thought they were acquaintances, a mutual friend or two in common, perhaps. Walking away, my mother leaned down and whispered to me, "Let's stop at Burr's on the way home and share a banana split for dinner, yeah?" Banana splits at Burr's was one of our things.

I had my first scoop of coffee ice cream at Burr's Fountain

on Folsom Boulevard. I had my first banana split there, too. It's where I learned what albacore was and came to prefer it to tuna fish even though I couldn't taste the difference. Fish covered in mayonnaise tastes like fish covered in mayonnaise. But I loved the way the letters in "albacore" rolled off my tongue. Good report cards got you a free ice-cream cone at the end of each semester. I had my kindergarten birthday party there. But it was just as much my mother's as it was mine. Mr. Burr knew us by name, and I think my mother felt like a better parent giving me a neighborhood place to return to again and again.

Every couple of months we'd slide into a booth about an hour before closing for a late banana-split dinner and a couple of Cokes. It was our time, and it was in those blue booths that I got to know my mom. She wasn't just a parent telling me what to do. She confided in me, and I confided in her, and I took it all extremely seriously. At that ice-cream parlor eating banana splits with my mom, we were friends.

I know I went to Burr's with my dad, too, because it was in the Burr's parking lot that he taught me how to spell the word "sandwiches." I must have been about six. The sign outside the restaurant advertised that they served ice cream as well as sandwiches. We had eaten lunch and were getting into the car when my father pointed to the word on the sign and asked me what it was. I said I didn't know. He said we weren't leaving until I figured it out. So I did. Slowly, letter by letter, I sounded it out and was so proud of myself when I said "sandwiches" aloud to him. Proud at least until a moment later when he responded, "Good. Now spell February." We were in that parking lot for a long time.

WHEN THE CHANGES in my dad came, they seemed to arrive overnight. I turned my head for only a moment, and when I turned back I didn't recognize him. He had been back in Sacramento for only a couple of years when his hair seemed to disappear. It got thin and silky but there was just so little of it—like infant hair. I found his hair everywhere but especially on the bathroom floor, where clumps stuck to the bottom of my bare, clammy feet. His body deflated like a popped balloon and his bones withered. I gave him a secret nickname: Hollow Man. He gave up driving. He no longer sat up straight. Pill bottles multiplied on his nightstand. After school, when I sat with him on his bed, I pretended to do my math homework but, really, I was watching him breathe, as if by watching I could keep his chest rising and falling forever.

Once, in the early evening, when the smell of medicine and sickness was especially strong, I lay down beside my father while he napped. I thought about a photo I'd taken of him. The year before I'd gotten a disposable camera on a trip with my cousins. When I got home, I had one picture left, and I made my father pose in the front yard. The man in that photo was supposedly the same man sleeping next to me now. But their bodies were different and so were their minds. They were the same in name, but different in all the ways that mattered. The changes in my father frightened me. I often felt more capable than him. We were on the same road but traveling in opposite directions. My father was going back, and I was going forward. Sometimes, it felt as though the more my father lost, the more I gained. This made me feel guilty, as though my growth and education came at his expense. I wanted to stand tall atop his shoulders, not from his grave.

That afternoon, as I watched him sleep, I took his hand. We had never held hands before, but it felt nice. I had no idea how long my father would live, and then it came to me all at once, so fast that I let go of his hand: in his mind he had been dead a long time. He was just waiting for his heart to catch up.

My father had told me he was gay and dying in one very

quick sentence—like he was ripping off a bandage, which, in a way, he was. At the time I was both too young to tie my shoe-laces and too young to understand his words. That sentence bounced around inside my head like a Ping-Pong ball for years until my vocabulary and maturity caught up with it. And then at school one morning in the middle of a quiz on multi-ples of seven, I got it. Seven times seven is forty-nine. My father likes men the way I like Johnny Depp. Seven times eight is fifty-six. My father is going to die and go away forever and forever. Seven times nine is sixty-three.

I joined my father's wait for his death. We were waiting together, but his death was going to mean such different things for each of us. For him, it would be a welcome end. For me, it would be a painful end as well as a welcome beginning, some-thing I never would have admitted at the time. I think my mother and I both felt trapped by my father's illness. We were all in so much pain. My father was miserable. Sometimes it felt like none of us were alive. This wasn't living. I wanted to be part of the world again, not on a deathwatch. On some level, I knew my father's death would be a new chapter for me. For the first time in my life, I'd get to define myself as something separate from him. Or so I thought. I had no idea how hard that would prove to be. When he woke up from his nap, I asked him if he wanted anything. He shook his head and turned on the TV to watch the news. Seven times ten is seventy.

MY MOTHER AND I didn't acknowledge what was happen-ing to us. But she made our home safe, and she gave me good memories that had nothing to do with my dad. When I was about seven, I read a book about a couple of kids whose father put a tent in their backyard so they could spend summer nights camped outside. I was enamored with this idea and spent weeks pestering my mom that we should do the same. She kept putting me off until finally she told me we could do it next week. Next week came and that Tuesday, as she tucked me into bed, I reminded her about her promise. It was late. Way past my bedtime. She said no. It wasn't a good night. She had work in the morning, and it was too late. She kissed me and turned out the light.

But not ten minutes later she burst into my bedroom and flipped on the light.

"All right! Let's do it!"

I sat up in bed.

"Really?

"Yeah! Why not?"

We'd never been camping. We didn't have a tent. We didn't even have sleeping bags. But it was a mild summer night, and we had plenty of sheets and pillows. It was almost midnight by the time we crawled into our makeshift bed in the middle of the backyard. But we did it. We spent the whole night sleeping side by side in the grass. We woke up at dawn covered in dew to find the cat sniffing at our heads. My mother looked like she had slept terribly. But she turned to me smiling. I loved waking up like that. Most mornings, my mom had to wake me repeatedly. By the time I finally stumbled out of bed, we were inevitably late. But that morning it was only sunrise; we had hours before she had to drop me off at summer school and go to work. So the three of us—my mom, the cat, and me—we took our time. We lay on the grass listening to the neighborhood wake up. We were late that morning, too, but we weren't rushed.

12

MY FATHER ANNOUNCED HE WAS GOING TO take me on a shopping spree for my ninth birthday. It was 1994, and he had already begun to tire easily, but mostly he was well enough. He called Nordstrom and spoke with one of the store's personal stylists, a woman I'll call Pamela. Of course a personal shopper would accompany us. This was my father's way. He valued service and accommodation and bells and whistles. He believed in extras not as something special but as something to expect: What is this retailer offering me that his competitor isn't? I sat at the foot of his bed and listened. I could hear her croaky voice through the phone. She sounded like a man.

"What's her size?" Pamela asked.

My father looked at me.

"Small," I said.

"She's a small," he said into the phone.

"What's her favorite color?"

My father looked at me again.

"Green."

"Really?" he asked, covering the phone's mouthpiece. "Are you sure?"

"Yessssss. Green."

"Green. She likes green. But she looks better in red. And black," he said to Pamela, not looking at me.

"She's almost nine."

He got that one on his own.

"One o'clock on Saturday, yes, that's fine. And you'll pick everything out ahead of time, so she can just try stuff on?"

We went to the Nordstrom Café for lunch first, and my father told me to try not to order off the kids' menu, because "didn't I think the kids' menu was awfully flavorless?" *Why, yes. Yes, I did.* Though I hadn't known I felt that way until just then. I ordered the Shrimp Louis salad with the Louis dressing, because I had noticed that adults seemed rather fond of shrimp cocktail, and I never saw *that* on a kids' menu. Shrimp was obviously sophisticated. Also my dad's name was Louis.

My father appeared dubious.

"Are you sure you want that?"

"Yeah. It sounds very full of flavor."

My father ordered a French dip, which made me think of the green onion dip my mom always made when we had company. I envisioned a bowl of dip served with something else French, like French fries, and I started regretting my shrimp. But when my salad came, it wasn't so bad. There was bacon. Although it turns out Louis dressing tastes a lot like mayonnaise. I ate as much as I could, because I was sure that if I didn't my father would say something about how he knew I wouldn't like it.

Pamela was waiting for us at the personal stylist desk. She was the most beautifully dressed old woman I'd ever seen. She was draped in silk the color of red wine, and she was wearing an enormous gold necklace that covered most of her chest like armor. Her cheeks were deflated and her hair was cut short, a stiff mass of curls the color of dirty snow. I picture her smoking, but of course she wouldn't have been. She was just one of those women who looked like they'd held a lot of cigarettes. Introductions were made. That's when the trouble started. Pamela did not in fact have any clothes picked out for me to try on, because she liked to "meet the girl first and get to know her a little before making any suggestions." What she actually wanted to do was to take us to the girls' department and shop. My father was not pleased. He had no interest in walking all over the store, moving from rack to rack, looking for sizes and comparing styles. He also knew he couldn't. He would get tired and need to rest. I knew what he had envisioned: a couch in a private room, a glass of wine or at least some sparkling water, and his daughter, still untouched by the awkwardness of puberty, twirling and spinning in clothes she didn't need.

"That is not what we agreed on the phone," he said to Pamela.

If there's one thing my father always knew, it was when someone else was wrong. Pamela had no idea what she was up against.

"This is how we do the first appointment. It allows me to get to know you and your daughter and your preferences."

"No. Your job is to shop so we don't have to."

"Why don't we try it my way this time, and next time we can try it your way? Come on, Victoria, we just got some really cute jumpers."

Pamela cocked her head to one side and pursed her lips. She was shorter than my father by several inches, and she stared hard into his chest, deeming him unworthy of eye contact. Then she swiveled and began walking toward the girls' department, confident we would follow. This was my father's cue to slam his palm down on the counter, stalk after her, and enlighten her in all the ways she was sorely mistaken. That is what he would have done in the past. No one was better at anger than my father. His fists beat the air in front of him soundlessly, but his words were loud and sharp and smacked you in the face like howling wind until your cheeks were red and chapped and your eyes welled. He had been escorted off airplanes and ordered out of restaurants and the lives of people he loved. My father was in a constant state of indignation that anything in his life should ever go wrong—he was already gay and dying and now, on top of all that, the Nordstrom personal shopper didn't do her job. How dare she. Every battle was worth fighting.

Except now, when I looked up at him, though his face was red and his fists were curled and he was shaking, he did nothing. "Follow her," he said tightly, and so I did. I heard him walking behind me, and I didn't know whether I should be relieved or anxious.

I had no interest in jumpers or anything else in the Nordstrom girls' clothing department. I wanted to shop at Brass Plum (BP)—the juniors' department with its wall of TVs blaring music videos, glass cases of rhinestone sunglasses, and rows of leopard-print headbands and spaghetti-strapped tank tops in shades of sherbet. But Pamela was hearing none of it and led me straight to a rack of plaid jumpers that were much too similar to my Catholic school uniform. My father stood behind me silently, but his anger filled the space around us the way an oven heats a kitchen.

Pamela threw him nervous glances over my head. His silence scared her. She was right to be afraid. His jaw and lips were rigid, and the skin on his forehead and around his eyes was taut, as if at any moment it might snap apart. He looked like a chained pit bull, ready to pounce if only he could free himself. I stood between them feeling the mayonnaise of the Louis dressing on the back of my tongue.

"What about this sweater?"

Pamela held up a bright pink sweater with a cat on it.

"Uh, that's a cat."

Pamela looked down.

"Well, yes . . . isn't it cute?"

"I want to go to BP."

"That's a little old for you, dear. Let's wait a few more birthdays before we start looking over there."

She swatted the air between us, and I noticed her finger-nails were painted a fleshy mauve. She held up another something pink. I shook my head, and my father spoke above me.

"Let her shop where she wants."

"Fine," Pamela snapped.

"I'm going to sit down on that bench."

We watched him go. He was furious, I knew, but, some-how, even though he hadn't even tried to fight, he looked as if he'd lost.

"What's *wrong* with him?" Pamela asked.

"Nothing," I replied, and left her there amid the pink cats. When she caught up with me I was already carrying a denim jacket and a sequin belt and a short black skirt that looked like it would give good twirl.

"Where's your mother?"

My mother, I thought, would not approve of my shopping in BP. She would have agreed with Pamela. This belt she would have dismissed as trashy and she would have thought the skirt was asking for trouble. I knew well from both the *Cosmopolitan* subscription my father had given me and his suggestion that I should start shaving my legs that he was nudging me out of childhood and into the hazy ether of adolescence. I knew this was wrong, but I think he just wanted a glimpse of the woman he would never have the chance to know.

I was only too happy to have his encouragement. Childhood hadn't done me any favors, and I was eager to be done with it. I'd long felt that I'd outgrown whatever youthful naiveté children are said to possess. In fact, I wasn't altogether sure if I had outgrown it or just never had it. What I did have was my father's credit card. This was my chance to dress the way I felt: old.

"My mother's at work," I replied.

"It's Saturday."

Pamela glanced back at my father and then at a saleswoman who I hadn't noticed was standing a few feet behind him. So they were watching him.

"You're at work," I said.

I hated Pamela and her flesh-colored nails. I didn't want to answer any more of her questions. I wanted to try on the denim jacket with the skirt and the belt and find some sort of tight, low-cut shirt to match, and I wanted a pair of hoop earrings and Doc Martens and a tube of that shimmery blueberry-flavored lip gloss. I wanted my father to send this *bitch* away.

I looked over at him again, checking on him. He was breathing heavily and leaning forward on the bench as if he were nauseous. The saleswoman behind him stepped forward and said something. She surprised him. He hadn't known she was there. He must have replied with something spiteful and probably a curse word or two, because her eyes turned to stone and her shoulders stiffened before she stormed away. Pamela had stepped away from me, too, and was talking quietly into some kind of walkie-talkie. I couldn't know for sure if she had seen what I'd seen, but I feared she had.

"Do you have any water? He needs a glass of water," I said.

"What is wrong with your father?"

"Nothing. He's tired."

She dumped the clothes I had picked out into the arms of one of the salesgirls and rushed away, her heels clicking angrily. I walked to my father and joined him on the bench.

"She's getting you some water."

"Are you having fun?"

I shrugged.

"Pick out whatever you want. We'll get it."

I wanted to model the clothes for him. I wanted him to tell me what he liked and what he thought we should get. I didn't want to do it by myself or with Pamela. Sometimes watching my father felt like watching a silent movie. His body was in an almost constant state of soundless movement. His chest rose and fell with force, his hands twitched, and the veins in his neck thumped as though his heart were in his throat. He was like a temperamental appliance that you really should have replaced years ago, but couldn't bear to part with and that mostly still got the job done, at least eventually.

Pamela came back with two security guards. No water.

"I think you should leave, sir. You're obviously upset and not well."

Now my father was irate. What had been bubbling beneath the surface erupted.

"What?! Why? I was just sitting here. This is ridiculous."

"You're disturbing our other customers, and I don't like your tone."

"I came here to buy my daughter some clothes for her birthday, and we are not leaving until she gets them."

He stood and shouted. If the other customers hadn't been disturbed before, they certainly were now. The guards stepped forward. My father leaned away, bumping the backs of his knees against the bench, and put his hands up.

"Let us buy the clothes. Then we'll leave. Please."

The guards looked at Pamela. They were huge, towering over all three of us. They could have easily swung both my father and me over their shoulders. Pamela looked at me.

"You can make the purchases, but that's it. Then I want you gone."

The five of us walked to the BP register and the salesgirl rang up the jacket and the belt and the skirt without ever making eye contact with my father or me. She dealt exclusively with Pamela. After my father's credit card had been swiped and he'd signed the receipt, Pamela handed me the shopping bag. I took it and stepped behind my father.

"Sir, these men will escort you out now."

"That won't be necessary."

"It's not up to you."

My father stepped toward Pamela.

"I will *never* come back here, and you can be sure that I will be making a formal complaint about your poor performance and the absolutely unacceptable way I've been treated."

"Step back, sir," said one of the guards.

My father ignored him and continued to shout.

"I know your first and last name."

The guard grabbed my father's arm, and when he tried to yank himself free the second guard took his other arm. His hairline shone with sweat, his face and neck were a deep shade of eggplant, and his breath was still more labored. But he was quiet and allowed the men to lead him down the escalator. I followed. It was Saturday afternoon and the first-floor makeup counters were crowded with weekend browsers. I watched from two steps above and behind as shoppers took notice of our entourage. The large guards stood like bookends on either side of my father, who by now was leaning heavily on the bigger of the two men. A sandy-haired man in a tuxedo was playing the baby grand piano, which was tucked away on a platform beside the escalator. I didn't recognize it then, but years later when I heard Nina Simone's cover of "Feeling Good," I recognized it as the song he'd been playing.

I wanted to scan the faces of the customers selecting eye shadows and those trying on spring sandals in the shoe department to ensure they were all strangers. But I kept my head down; I didn't want to spot a familiar face. Then what would I do? Wave? I was afraid to look up. I was afraid to see the way these people might be looking at my father: like he had a gun, or worse, like he wasn't dangerous at all, just pathetic. I felt alienated enough already.

The guards stopped outside, and I assumed they would release my father. Instead they asked him where his car was. He didn't remember. The car was in the garage on the first floor near another entrance around the corner. "We're in the garage," I said. Both guards turned around and looked down at me. They seemed surprised to see me. Now it was I who led. At our car only one of the guards let go of my father. The other kept his grip firm as my father fumbled for his keys. A part of me wanted him to get mad again, to do something. Anything would have been better than watching him struggle to unlock the car one-handed. I took the keys and opened the driver's door. At last the second guard released him. No one spoke. My father shut his door with as much force as he could muster, and I hurried to the other side to get in beside him. The guards watched him back out. They stood there still even as he accelerated out of the garage and around the corner, not bothering to pause at the stop sign.

He took the back exit, which dumped us out onto a residential side street. He made a hard left instead of a right, which was the direction of home. We were going so fast. I hadn't thought he had the energy for fast anymore. Then I understood. He came to a halt against the curb in front of a stucco apartment complex. He threw the emergency brake on and slumped against the steering wheel. He hadn't had the energy, after all. His pride had given him false strength. But we were out of sight now, and he could no longer pretend. I sat very still beside him. The Nordstrom bag was open at my feet. I looked at the sequin belt lying on top and felt stupid. That was the type of belt you wore to a party. I didn't know what party I thought I was going to.

My arms felt heavy in my lap. I wanted to hug him, but I knew he wouldn't want me to. I wanted to say something, but

I knew he wouldn't want me to. Eventually, he sat up. He examined his face in the rearview mirror, smoothing his eyebrows with his fingertips. He started the car and drove. We were silent. The barren parking lots and strip malls of suburbia gave way to shade and grass and formidable houses as we drove back into the city and the old neighborhood. We were home. My father went into his bedroom and shut the door. I abandoned the shopping bag on the living room couch and went into my own room.

I knew that night when my mother came to pick me up he would tell her the story, reliving it, getting angrier and angrier. *The nerve! Those people! They had no right! Worthless, stupid, all of them!* But he and I would never speak of it again. It wasn't our story. It wasn't something that had happened to us. It was his story. It had happened to him. He owned the incident now and would spin it and re-spin it, working himself up over and over again. I, on the other hand, didn't want it. We were opposite this way. I didn't want to talk about it or relive it or brand it in some way as my property. I wanted to forget it. I wanted it not to have happened. We wouldn't talk about it again, because what my father longed for was a new audience who could accept his version blindly. But I had been there, and so I was no good to him as a listener.

Late that night, after she had heard the story, tried to calm my father, and taken me home to her house, my mother came into my bedroom with the shopping bag.

"You're not wearing these. Absolutely not. I'm taking them back."

She was ready for a battle and she was right to be. Normally, I would have fought her. Not this time.

"Mom. I don't want them."

The next day she returned the clothes. I turned nine.

13

I WAS ONLY DISTANTLY AWARE THAT MY FATHER and Steve slept together. He was often home when I arrived to visit my dad, but then he'd retreat. He must have had things in that house—a toothbrush, cologne, CDs, clothes—but either I assumed they were my father's belongings or over time I blocked from my mind whatever those intimate items might have been. Steve and I came and went, taking turns keeping my father company and avoiding one another. When I went back to my mother's, I knew instinctively that Steve returned.

Steve was the tallest Hispanic I had ever seen. He was young, too—maybe a full decade younger than my father. Steve had been raised in Mexico but fled to San Jose, California, in his late teens with his wife and young daughter. It was only after he and my father met and fell in love that he finally left his marriage. It was clear that my father was in love; he was soft with Steve. He looked at him with longing and unnerving concentration and bought him orchids and held his hand. He cooked elaborate meals involving overnight preparations. When I got up in the middle of the night for water, the kitchen counter and refrigerator shelves were often cluttered with platters and bowls filled with mysterious concoctions of meats and herbs and brown sauces and pale yogurts doing not much of anything as far as I could tell but which my father assured me were *marinating* and *melding their flavors*. These dinners culminated with lit candles and handwritten menus laid at each place setting, and I was most definitely a third wheel, though then I wouldn't have known how to describe it, aware only that not everyone was enamored to have me.

My mother and I were reminders of my father's other life, the one in which he had been closeted and unhappy and believed that romance and passion would never be possible for him. Steve gave my father an understanding of what his life could have been like all along had he been born thirty years later or perhaps never met my mother. My father's relationship with Steve excluded me, and I didn't understand why Steve was necessary. My mom and dad weren't people; they were *my parents*. They were everything to me, and I believed it was supposed to work the other way, too.

To Steve, I was interfering in all of his relationships. I came between him and my dad, and I reminded him of his own daughter, with whom he had a tense relationship. I was a reminder of his other life before when he had also felt trapped and miserable. My father thought he had finally found someone he could love and be loved by. But he and Steve were still saddled with the consequences of their previous lives and by HIV, which they also shared. I was too young to understand that their romance was supposed to be a respite from everything that had gone wrong.

Steve frightened me. On the infrequent occasions when we were both at home, he spent most of his time in the backyard smoking cigarettes. I always knew when he had recently been in a room just by the lingering scent of his Parliaments. As a child, I thought of him always with a trail of smoke following behind him as though he were on fire. The longest conversation we ever had was when I was about seven years old.

He and my father were living in Sacramento by then, and I often showed up unannounced—after swim practice or before dinner for a snack—fully aware that my unexpected arrivals were a point of friction between Steve and my dad, and that my dad would never tell me not to come. On one such occasion, I found a letter addressed to someone named Jesus on the dining room table, and I asked Steve what he was doing with Jesus' letter.

"It's not Jesus. It's 'Hay Soos.' That's how you pronounce it in Spanish."

"Then who's *Hay Soos?*" I asked.

"Me. But I go by Steve."

And that was that. He left the room, done with our conversation, and I spent the next decade under the impression that Steve was a nickname for Jesus.

STEVE WAS A connoisseur of extravagance who wore silk with buttery soft leather loafers when taking out the trash. He drove a lipstick-red convertible Miata roadster and worked as a manager at a bank, because he liked money. Monday through Friday he was gone all day, and when I came over after school, I had my father to myself. But at five-thirty, with unwavering precision, Steve walked through the door, and I knew that no matter what my father and I had been doing together—talking, watching TV, reading *A Wrinkle in Time*, playing Super Mario Brothers 3 on my Nintendo—we were done. Steve was home. That was the only context in which Steve existed for me. He was the interrupter.

I thought of Steve as little as possible. He was immaterial, and when I try to conjure him now I see only a cigarette between two brown fingers, all skin and bone without an ounce of excess flesh, and the outline of an angular face, the particulars of which are obscured by smoke.

But for my father, Steve was everything. He made my father happy. It was obvious. Steve was also a great observer of people, and together they sat at outdoor cafés drinking wine, talking to one another in low voices and watching straight, healthy people rush by. They shared good food, and they knew how to move together; when they walked side by side their hips swayed in tandem. It was like watching a tango. With Steve, my father could be free. He could forget his past as well as his future. Steve was the present, and what a gorgeous present it was.

My father and Steve may have shared an HIV diagnosis, but my father was sick, and Steve was not. We knew this, but all of us preferred to look the other way. It started slowly. On a bike ride when my father turned back a couple of miles early, I just shrugged. So what, he didn't feel like riding any more that day. I came home from school, and my father was napping. So what, my mom had been known to take naps. Overcome by a coughing fit, my dad left the table in the middle of dinner, leaving me and Steve alone and helpless, listening to him hack up phlegm over the bathroom sink. So what, something must have gone down his throat funny. That was all.

Once, my father, after having insisted on cooking all afternoon, collapsed into bed without eating. Steve and I ate by ourselves. We ate like strangers, which, despite knowing each other's names and taking towels from the same linen closet and sharing a set of house keys, we were. The meal passed without the exchange of a single word, and yet, somehow, it was okay. We weren't vying for my father's attention, and I was surprised to realize that I felt comfortable in Steve's presence.

Less than a month later, though, he was gone.

Steve may have been HIV positive, but he was still strong and his relative health allowed him to pretend that he could outrun what my father had not. He didn't want to think about a future of pills and bedpans and night sweats and the odor of a body too weak to bathe. My father had his bad days and his good days. He would have a sick spell, and then he would pull out of it and surprise us with a lemon chiffon tart and Steve would forgive him. But my father was getting sicker and the bad days began to outnumber the good. When Steve woke up and looked across his pillow at my father he was looking into his future, and what a bleak future it was. My father's worsening condition brought all of Steve's fears about his own health to the surface.

No longer could my father cook elaborate meals or go dancing at the gay bars they frequented with their friends. Suddenly, Steve was expected to be a caregiver for his older, sicker lover, and seemingly all of a sudden the man who had whisked him away from a faithless union with the mother of his child was no longer his knight in shining armor. I suspect that my father always knew that Steve would not be up to the challenge of caring for him, but I think he wanted to be wrong. I think he hoped that Steve would surprise him. But he didn't. Steve began to drop insinuations that my father had let him down, making such comments more and more frequently as well as blatantly as the months wore on. My father, in turn, responded with more and more heat and hurt.

Curt comments and statements posed as questions seemingly about nothing led to shouting, slammed doors, and suffocating silence.

"Weren't you going to get milk?"

"You're going to stay in this weekend again, aren't you?"

"What do you do all day?"

They argued at first only when they were home alone. Sometimes, however, I would be there, too. Usually I was in my room, hearing them through the walls, and it seems likely now that they simply forgot I was there. Later, after tension and resentment had become their strongest bond, they argued frequently, regardless of who was around to hear—neighbors, the mailman, my mother as she dropped me off or picked me up.

When Steve finally disappeared, he left behind a shiner on my father's left eye and cheekbone. Neither my father nor my mother mentioned the newly bare drawers in my father's closet or the clean ashtrays or the way one side of my father's bed was now free and cool to the touch. No one mentioned the black eye, either. The bruise lasted a long time, for more than a week, and I started to think it wasn't a bruise but a permanent scar. Eventually it lost shape and shade, fading from ebony to indigo to magenta to a sickly greenish yellow that brought to mind dying grass. Then it was as gone as Steve, who none of us ever heard from again.

Once I caught my father in the bathroom having abruptly stopped brushing his teeth mid-task. The toothbrush and foamy paste hung out of his mouth, and he was standing close to the mirror. He didn't notice me. He was looking at his vanishing bruise, and it appeared to me that he was inspecting it with regret as if he wanted it to stay, as if he wanted a reminder of Steve tattooed on his face. He was lovesick. In the beginning of his relationship with Steve he had resembled an adolescent experiencing love for the first time, and now, in the months that followed their ending, he returned to an adolescent state, only this time as a boy having his first acquaintance with love abandoned. He sulked and seemed not to hear you when you spoke to him. He had no interest in food, the newspaper, television, or whether it was gray or sunny outside. Having a conversation with him was a lot like talking to yourself. It scared me. It scared me that romantic love could do that to a person. I was unaccustomed to the sight of someone breaking down. Certainly, my mother never had.

*   *   *

I FOUND STEVE'S wife and daughter after two years of looking.

It wasn't easy. Their names are very common, and I found teenage girls, young mothers, middle-aged women, and even men who shared their first and last names. I wrote two letters to the wrong people—both of whom were kind enough to let me know my mistake. I sent another letter. In these notes, I asked if they remembered my dad. If Steve's daughter knew anything about our fathers' relationship. I wanted to know what she felt, if we felt anything the same. My third letter reached Steve's wife. She gave it to her daughter, who eventually wrote me back in elegant handwriting on a lovely piece of stationery—hand-painted with gold foil flowers.

She has written on this pretty paper that she is sorry my dad died. That it is hard to write me, because I bring back hard memories. My father's relationship with hers was "the straw that broke the camel's back" in her parents' marriage. She did meet my dad, but she no longer remembers him because "it was easier to try and just forget." She sympathizes. Her father committed suicide in 2004, and she tells me, "I know a lot of his pain was from the loss of your father."

Long after I had given up hope of hearing back, her letter arrived in a pink envelope. Not one of those slick, shiny Hallmark envelopes but a smaller one with a rich, almost grainy texture. I came home to it one evening. It was waiting for me in my mailbox in my building lobby. I held it out in front of me as I got on the elevator. I knew who it was from.

A neighbor got on with me and said, "That sure looks important!" He said it in a friendly, jovial manner, as if he were remarking on good weather.

I looked up at him, dazed.

"Yeah. Uh, it's from my dad's ex-boyfriend's daughter."

"Oh. Whoa. I'm . . . Didn't mean to . . ."

"No, no. It's okay. It's a good thing. I think."

My neighbor was right. It was an important piece of mail. Her words meant a great deal to me and I was grateful that she had taken the time to write what had clearly been a difficult letter. I was sorry that her dad had died, too. In the same way. Two HIV-positive men who took their own lives. They were two of many, I know. When I was an adolescent with acne, bad hair, an unfortunate fondness for overalls and chokers, and a deep ache in my belly for my father, I had been angry with him for leaving early. He could have stayed longer, I thought. But by the time he decided to die, he was already dead in his heart. It was right that he didn't wait around for his body to catch up to what his mind already knew.

I was sorry that Steve had been so unhappy. It was much worse to know that they had both suffered. At least Steve had loved my dad after all. My dad was loved. I had never thought about what Steve must have left behind when he moved in with my dad and came to Sacramento. He had chosen my dad and, by extension, me, over his own daughter. I knew the pain of losing a father better than any other pain, and yet, here I was, a small piece of the chain that took this woman's father away from her. Worse, I'd never thought about it with anything but a child's perspective, and never had the sensitivity to realize it.

I had always known Steve had a daughter. I met her. Once. The same time she met my father. Although, clearly, she didn't remember me. Why should she? She and a friend came to Santa Cruz for the day. She must have been fifteen. Maybe sixteen. They had driven themselves. One of them had a license. I thought they were so cool. They parked in back and lingered only long enough for introductions. Then they split for the boardwalk. I desperately wanted to be invited to join them. I watched them sashay around the corner, two pretty girls with long dark hair shiny against their backs and bare arms. After they left, I hung around glumly on the stoop until Steve came out. He looked toward the end of the block where his daughter had just disappeared. "I should have suggested they take you. You could've tagged along without interrupting their hunt for cute boys."

I don't remember anything else about her visit, but I remember her eagerness to get to the boardwalk. To get away from us. I had assumed she wanted to leave because she was a teenager, and who wants to hang out with their parents when they can hang out with their peers on the beach? It never occurred to me that there might have been a whole other world of reasons she didn't want to meet me or my dad or see her father with us. I was just jealous that she could so easily walk away.

I FOUND DANIEL in Singapore. It was easy. Tucked inside my father's date book was Daniel's business card. The San Francisco number and address had been abandoned—cut off—but he was still an engineer for the same company he started with as a twenty-two-year-old. Only now he was on the other side of the world. An operator in San Francisco gave me his new number. Just like that. No questions asked. I tacked it up on the bulletin board above my desk. I looked at it for three weeks.

In all that time, I managed only the courage to call my father's friend Marion. We spoke by phone, she on the West Coast and me in New York City. I had met Marion a few times when I was a child, but the last time I had seen her was at my father's memorial service. She wore a long flowered dress with short sleeves that was belted at the waist. She gave an eloquent eulogy. Fourteen years later she was no less eloquent on the subject of my father.

They worked together for a time.

"We hit it off almost immediately. I remember in meetings, you'd see an eyebrow lift from across the table. No bullshit.

That was your dad. He often spoke with his eyebrows. I liked that."

"I remember that, too," I said.

One eyebrow could say so many things depending on just how it was cocked: *Give me a break. I can do better than that. Oh you think so, do you? Wrong!*

I found myself nodding along as she spoke.

"He was very logical, but that logic didn't always make him good on a personal level. People who operated on an emotional level were an anathema to him."

In fourth grade, I got into a fight with a friend at school. I came home to my father's house crying. He listened to my sorry tale through rivulets of tears and snot. When I finished, he handed me a box of tissues and said, "No one can ever make you cry. You choose to cry." The next time I allowed myself to cry in front of my father, he was in a coma, and I knew he'd never wake up.

It wasn't that my father couldn't be emotional. He could, but more often than not when emotion rushed out of him it did so in frustration and anger. Sometimes he was frustrated and angry at a situation or a person. Other times, I think he was mostly just frustrated and angry with himself.

"You could see the negative energy inside of him when he was upset. His whole body would tense, and he would shake."

Yes, I knew; I remember that, too, and it had made me afraid.

"I don't remember us fighting, really. Well, we had one fight once."

"What did you fight about?" I asked.

"He was afraid I wanted more."

"That you wanted a romantic relationship with him?"

"Yes. I think so."

"Did you?"

"I knew he was gay."

I didn't push her. I didn't point out that she hadn't answered my question. I didn't point out that knowing he was gay didn't mean she didn't wish he wasn't. Didn't mean she didn't hope for a romantic relationship with him. I didn't remind her that she was in good company and that she wasn't the first woman to fall for an unavailable man. At least she wasn't writing a whole book about it.

Later, my mother told me that, according to my father, Marion came on to him. She wanted them to be together. But even before I knew this, I heard the evasion in Marion's voice. I let it go, because it wasn't my business, and she certainly didn't have to tell me anything she didn't want to. She was doing me a favor. I knew she wanted to share my father with me, but that didn't mean she wanted to also share herself.

Marion changed the subject back to work.

"He would get so angry with people who couldn't deliver on time. He would say something very abruptly."

She paused.

"There was some feeling I had for him. But who knows what it was."

Silence. I didn't fill it, but I so wished she and I were sitting side by side. I wanted to see the look on her face as she spoke. I had realized long ago that my father spent his life playing an elaborate and exhausting game of elusion. But I had, naively, been unprepared to face evasion from his survivors.

She began again. She told me about this image she had in her mind of him wearing a vintage army uniform. They had gone to an old movie theater together in San Jose. For decades the theater had shown pornos. But then sometime in the early nineties it was converted back into a movie theater for independent films. Marion and my father had gone to the opening, where guests were encouraged to wear period costumes. He'd found army-issue khakis and even the matching hat. "Just like in everything else, he paid such meticulous attention to detail. The creases in his pants were so sharp you could have sliced a piece of bread with them."

Marion spoke of a man I both did and didn't recognize. The anger, the frustration, the eyebrows, they all fit, but she spoke about him and these traits from a perspective, from a place, I didn't know. He had been a whole person to her. A friend. An intimate. This search for him suddenly felt like a coloring book full of drawings. Every one of them my father, but all outlines. Marion was coloring one in now and the picture emerging was like a familiar face on the street you can't quite place.

"He was so in love with Steve. But you know Steve didn't really believe that people are gay. He used to tell your dad that neither of them was really gay."

I hadn't known that. They had lived together, had built some semblance of a life together, yet Steve had refused to acknowledge it was real. Steve couldn't feel it or be committed to their life the way my father had been. He had kept his distance. Not unlike the way my father had kept his own distance in his marriage to my mother.

"Your dad was tortured by that."

How could he not be? I thought.

"Oh, your dad really wanted people to like him. One morning when I was visiting him in Santa Cruz we went on a walk for coffee, and on the way we passed an elderly man. He smiled at us and said, 'Good morning. Isn't it a beautiful day?' And your dad turned to me and said, 'That never happens when I'm by myself. Why is it that no one ever says hello like that to me?'"

I never knew my father wanted people to like him. I thought he didn't care. That no-bullshit cocked-eyebrow thing. I had taken it all at face value. But of course. Of course he cared. He married my mother, because he cared. All that distance from everyone was a smoke screen. He didn't want people to know his secret. To think less of him. Who or what would my father have been like if he had grown up in a community and a larger society where being gay wasn't a bad thing? What if he, and not I, had been born in the 1980s? I wish I could have traded places with him.

"A coldness, an aloofness, emanated from him. He wasn't open to that kind of casual friendliness. He asked that question more to himself than to me, I think. He said it in a sort of wistful way. Maybe if Steve's feelings about himself and your dad and their relationship had been different . . . maybe over time your dad would have become more comfortable with the softness inside him. And he did have softness inside him. But he never would have been Alan Alda, sorry."

Marion had seen his softness. He had been a good friend to her. She was upset—about what, she didn't say—and she went to see him in Santa Cruz. They sat beside each other on the steps of his spiral staircase, and he hugged her as she cried.

"That was one of the few times I can think of when he was physically affectionate. He wasn't one to greet you with a hug or a pat on the back or grab you by your hand."

I hadn't known that she knew about Daniel, but she did.

"Did my dad ever talk about his time abroad in college?"

"Oh, your father had a wonderful time in Sweden with Daniel."

When she mentioned him, I was surprised. I'd have thought my father would have kept Daniel to himself. I asked her if she had ever met Daniel.

"No, your father was pretty much a loner. He didn't let paths cross. He was undercover, you could say."

But he had told her about Daniel.

"He regretted that he and Daniel hadn't been more."

More what, I wanted to know. But she didn't elaborate.

"I just know he had a lot of regret about Daniel."

I stared at Daniel's phone number as she spoke. I wanted to call. I wanted him to tell me how happy they'd been together, to tell me the larks they had together, to explain to me what my father had been thinking in the months before he married my mother.

14

THE BODEGA HAD TWENTY DIFFERENT PHONE cards on display behind the cash register. All of them were brightly colored and cluttered with cartoons. They differed only in name and dollar amount. I had no idea which one to buy, but I needed one because my cell phone didn't have international service. The clerk was getting antsy. *Pick one. Pick one.* I chose a blue one. The yellow cartoon dog on the front was wearing a red cape and posing in front of the Brooklyn Bridge. It was the "New York Hero" phone card. I could use a hero.

I called Daniel's work number on a Sunday evening when I knew I wouldn't have to speak to him. I wanted to give us both time to prepare, but that explanation came only later. What I thought as I began to dial was that I had been making excuses not to call for weeks and yes, it was a Sunday and might have made more sense to wait until Monday, but if I didn't call during this brief moment of courage I might never call.

My hero phone card didn't ring. I followed the automated directions and before I knew it I was listening to a voice mail greeting. No ringing. No pause. No chance for a deep breath. I had missed the first half of the message; there was no hello, no title or business acknowledged, just a man's voice saying

"—iel Chen" and suggesting the caller leave a message. Then came the beep. I was flustered and wished I had written down what I wanted to say. I told the machine who I was, that I was looking for the Daniel Chen who knew my father, Louis Loustalot. I said I would like very much to talk to him about my dad. I left my number and e-mail address and hung up. I opened a bottle of wine.

Daniel e-mailed me the next day to say he would call me that night. His message was clipped and formal but unfailingly polite:

> I received your voice message this morning from my work phone. And, yes, I knew your father well. He was my roommate in Berkeley. I met you in late 1995 when I visited your home in Sacramento while your father was very ill. I will give you a call your Monday night around 9:30pm.

On the phone he was reserved, but his voice was smooth and kind and had none of the brusqueness of his e-mail. *I knew your father extremely well, yes.* No one had ever said that to me. No one else believed they knew him. In my mother's words, *there was just so much he couldn't share.* But he had shared with Daniel. Or at least Daniel thought so. *He was your father, so I will tell you what you want to know.* Our conversation was brief. *I have a meeting now, but let us talk again. E-mail me your questions.*

I e-mailed him almost as soon as we hung up:

> Hi, Daniel.
> Thank you again for responding so quickly to my message and calling on Monday night. It means a lot to me. Out of everyone who ever knew my father, you may have known him the most intimately. Because of that, your thoughts and feelings about my dad are important to me . . .

I worried that when he read my questions he would reconsider. This was his history and his private life as much as my father's. He didn't owe me anything. What right did I have to ask him about his relationship with my father? It was none of my business what they had talked about, what they had shared, or why they had drifted apart. But he wrote back the next day, saying he would answer my questions first in an e-mail and then we could talk again by phone. I was relieved. But then I didn't hear from him for two months. I hesitated to reach out again, not wanting to push him but the whole time wanting him to answer me. Every time I checked my e-mail I hoped to see his name in my inbox. Another week went by. Maybe he had reconsidered after all. Had decided my questions about the nature of his relationship with my father were too much. There might be something in particular he didn't want to talk about. The only time our phone conversation had faltered was when I mentioned Sweden. He would say only, *That was a long time ago.*

BEN WAS STRUGGLING, too. "I'm crazy about you. But you have to understand that William is my friend." I did understand. I had no idea how I would react if William fell in love with one of my friends. But our breakup had snapped me out of whatever feelings I had had for him. I had been distancing myself from him for months, I saw that now. Ben felt right. He made me feel solid. I had never fallen so hard or so fast. My feelings scared me, but I also couldn't bring myself to walk away from him. With him, everything was easy. The uneasy part was everyone around us. "I don't know if I can do this," Ben said. In fact, he couldn't. He wrote me an e-mail to say that although he loved me and wanted to be with me, now was not the time. Maybe six months from now, he suggested. He hoped we could still be friends.

We agreed to meet for drinks late the next night to talk one last time in person. I arrived first and sat in the bar's empty back room with a scotch and my schoolwork. Not that I read a thing. The bar's ATM was near my table and a twenty-something guy came back for cash. He asked me what I was working on and sat down across from me. He was cute and sweet, but I kept thinking of Ben. Mostly that I hoped he would walk in while we were talking. And he did. He came up behind our table, standing very close.

"Excuse me," Ben said.

The guy stood quickly, startled.

"It was nice to meet you," he said.

I agreed, and he fled back to the bar. Ben took his seat.

"Who was that?"

I shrugged.

We looked at each other.

"It's like moths to a flame around you."

I shrugged again.

He reached for my hand across the table.

"This sucks."

I nodded.

"You and William only broke up a few months ago."

I didn't say anything, and after a moment, Ben continued.

"I think he needs more time."

"You want more time," I replied.

"Look, maybe we can be something next spring . . ."

I shook my head and said, "I'm not going to wait around for you to decide it's a good time for you and William."

It was his turn to nod. But I wasn't done.

"You want me to hold my breath for the next six months? You're asking me to wait, but how do I know your promise is a good one? How do I know that in six months you won't say, 'Oh, I still need more time'? I don't want to be jerked around. If you don't feel comfortable pursuing something with me because of William, I respect that. I can accept it. But I'm not going to wait for you."

Ben let go of my hand. "Can we be friends at least?"

I shrugged. "What kind of friendship would that be? We write e-mails. We see each other. We share meals. We go to the movies. Sounds like dating to me, only we won't be holding hands or kissing or having sex. We'll just be confused and sad at the end of the night when we go home alone again. I'll be wrapped up thinking about you and won't be able to move on. In spite of myself, I'll still be waiting for you . . . No. I need a clean break. We either do this or we go our separate ways."

In a moment of weakness the week before, Ben had invited me to be his date at his friend's wedding. Now the wedding was in just a few days.

"I still want you to come to the wedding with me. But *nothing* will happen. Nothing."

I thought about it. I found it hard to believe nothing would happen at a wedding of all places. But maybe it would be a test. If we could go to a wedding with an open bar and have a good time as platonic friends, then we could do anything. I took a sip of my scotch.

"Okay. Let's go to the wedding."

Ben walked me home. He held my hand. Some friends we were. On my stoop he hugged me good night.

"I'll see you Saturday," he said.

I asked him what I should wear to this wedding. He shrugged.

"Whatever you want. You look good in everything."

Complimentary but supremely unhelpful—he sounded like a boyfriend already.

AT LAST, DANIEL e-mailed me back. Whatever warmth he had initially granted me was gone. But he did answer my questions—with a bulleted list in all caps like he was giving me a customs form before landing at the airport:

How did you and my father meet?

- ◆ I MET YOUR FATHER IN AN SF BAR WHICH HASN'T BEEN IN BUSINESS FOR MANY YEARS.
- ◆ AT THE TIME I WAS IN MY FINAL YEAR AT CAL.
- ◆ WE BECAME FRIENDS, AND WHEN WE WERE BOTH LOOKING FOR A PLACE TO RENT IN BERKELEY, WE DECIDED TO BE ROOMMATES.

Did you and my dad have any mutual friends?

- ◆ WE DID NOT HAVE ANY MUTUAL FRIENDS. HE HAD HIS FRIENDS AND I HAD MINE. LOUIS DID GET TO KNOW A COUPLE OF MY FRIENDS.

Did you see my dad's apartment in Sweden? Did you meet any of his friends there?

- ◆ LOUIS LIVED IN THE DORM AND I STAYED WITH HIM DURING THE FEW DAYS I WAS IN STOCKHOLM. HE HAD MY PICTURE PINNED ON THE WALL.
- ◆ I MET A FEW OF HIS UNIVERSITY FRIENDS, SOME SWEDISH AND SOME AMERICANS OF BOTH SEXES. LOUIS WAS WELL LIKED BY ALL. WE ATTENDED A DINNER PARTY THROWN BY HIS FRIENDS THE NIGHT BEFORE OUR DEPARTURE SOUTH. IT WAS A DINNER OF STEAMED MUSSELS IN WINE AND BROTH, AND BREAD WITH PLENTY OF WINE TO DRINK. LOU LOVED WINE. IT HAS BEEN A LONG TIME AND I DO NOT REMEMBER ANY OF THEIR NAMES AND HAVE NOT SEEN ANY OF THEM SINCE.

Which countries and cities did you and my dad visit once you left Sweden?

> • I CANNOT REMEMBER THE CHRONOLOGICAL OR-
> DER OF OUR VISIT BUT WE SPENT TIME IN CO-
> PENHAGEN, AMSTERDAM, FRANKFURT, LILLE,
> PARIS. WE WANTED TO CROSS THE CHANNEL TO
> LONDON BUT RAN OUT OF TIME.

Was it known among any of his friends in Stockholm or Berkeley that he was gay or bisexual or at all uncertain about his sexuality?

> • NO. HE HAD FRIENDS OF BOTH SEXES AND HAD
> BEDDED BOTH. HE WAS A SEXUAL PERSON. HE
> WAS HANDSOME AND HAD A NICE BODY AND HE
> ENJOYED THE ATTENTION OF OTHERS.

> • FOR ONE OF HIS ART PROJECTS IN BERKELEY
> WHICH WAS TO DO A PIECE THAT WILL STOP
> TRAFFIC, HE WENT NAKED INTO THE FOUNTAIN
> BY THE STUDENT UNION AFTER SUDSING UP
> THE WATER. I DID NOT SEE THE SHOW, HE TOLD
> ME ABOUT IT AFTERWARDS.

I suspect that my dad may have been in love with you, at least at one time. Were his feelings ever reciprocated? Was there ever anything between the two of you besides platonic friendship?

> • MAYBE WE WERE IN LOVE AT THE TIME. WE EN-
> JOYED DOING THINGS TOGETHER. HE TOLD ME
> HE ENJOYED TALKING WITH ME. MAYBE BE-
> CAUSE I WAS THE ONE LOSING IN OUR ARGU-
> MENTS.

My dad turned twenty-one in Stockholm; a mere two years later, at the age of twenty-three, he married my mom. Did you two ever talk about his being gay? What did he say?

• EVEN WHEN I WAS WITH HIM, HE HAD A GIRL-
FRIEND AND HAD SEX WITH HER.

Did you see my dad regularly when he was working in San
Jose and living in Santa Cruz? What did you do together?

• NO. I RARELY SAW HIM WHEN HE WAS IN SAN
JOSE. I KNEW HE MET AND WAS INVOLVED WITH
ANOTHER MAN DURING THIS PERIOD. THIS MAN
ALSO SUCCUMBED TO AIDS.

• AS I REMEMBER AND RESPOND TO YOUR QUES-
TIONS, I FEEL A CERTAIN SADNESS. LOUIS WAS
SO FULL OF LIFE AND INTERESTS. HE WAS EX-
CITING TO BE WITH. HE LOVED HIS FAMILY AND
I KNOW HE LOVED YOUR MOTHER AND YOU VERY
MUCH. UNFORTUNATELY, HE WAS RECKLESS. I
THINK HE FANCIED BEING A ROCK STAR WITH
ITS CONNOTATION OF DRUGS AND SEX, AND BE-
ING ADORED.

Did Daniel adore him? I thought of their time together. I
thought of them going to the movies and going out for dinner.
I thought of them in debate, of Daniel losing arguments to
my father. I knew that feeling. To know my dad was to admit
defeat, but it was okay, because when you were losing and he
was winning, you had his attention, and it felt like a rock star
noticing you in the mosh pit. As a little girl, I had been selfish
about my dad. I wanted him to be mine. My father could be
selfish, too. He was protective of anything he considered his.
He was private, closed with his things and the things he did.
Yet he had pinned a photograph of Daniel to his bedroom
wall. He never had personal photographs displayed in the
bedrooms I had known—not in Santa Cruz, not in Sacramento. In Sweden, he had kept fewer secrets.

I craved information. I wanted to know more. I wanted to know everything. My father had loved wine. I never knew that. Daniel had called him Lou. I liked that. It suggested closeness, tenderness, and I so hoped my father had had those things. I hoped Daniel had given them to him, that when he called my father Lou, my father had known love. Daniel and my father's trip from Stockholm to Paris—I could do that trip. I could spend New Year's in Paris. Sexual person. Rock star. Adoration. Exciting. Reckless. I understood these parts of my father. I had never seen them in him, but I recognized them nonetheless. This was the same man who refused to wear a watch, so he'd always have an excuse to make conversation with someone pretty. The Lou that Daniel described reminded me of something my father did just a few weeks before he died. We were alone at his house, and it must have been in the afternoon on a school day, because I had on my school uniform. My father asked me to rerecord the greeting on his answering machine. He had it all written out, and he told me to say it like I was Marilyn Monroe, baby-voiced and full of breath. We practiced a few times, and when he was satisfied, I recorded it: *Louisssssss isn't in. Wait for the mooaan, if you want to leave a messssssage.* Followed by me moaning, which I had never done before. My father forbid me from answering the phone, so that as many callers as possible could hear our recording. My mother was not amused.

Exciting, sexual rock-star person. Daniel's version of my father was not so dissimilar from parts of the life I had been leading as a single woman in New York City: dating a rotating cast of interchangeable men. But I didn't want to be a rock star. I didn't want to follow my father down that path. I wanted to follow his other path, the one he had abandoned; the path of the man who spent New Year's Eve in Paris with someone he loved.

15

I T ISN'T PARIS. IT ISN'T NEW YEAR'S EVE. AND there is no lover. It's Newark. New Jersey. The airport.

The Swedish flight attendants are sturdy and pale like large glass bottles of milk. They wear their hair in thick blond buns, and they hover at the gate giggling and waving at flight attendants at neighboring gates. For the first time in all the years I've believed that Sweden meant something to my father, I am struck by the irony of this. How in 1972 a twenty-year-old bisexual college kid with dark hair and flailing limbs found acceptance and freedom in a tiny, homogeneous, and very blond country.

But it isn't just the flight attendants. Everyone waiting for this flight is either blond or should be blond; a few have dyed their hair, but it looks like tar, so dark and shiny it's obvious the naturally golden locks are still shimmering beneath all that dye.

Everyone is tall, and the women's breasts are huge in a way that makes them seem healthy and strong. They are neat. Everything is tucked in and crisp. They make me think of hospital corners. Like things are being taken care of. Everything will be okay.

There's a layover in Iceland, and by the time we land in

Stockholm it's morning, and I am exhausted. I take a cab to a friend's apartment. Astri and I went to graduate school together, but Stockholm is her home. I had e-mailed her asking for hotel suggestions, but she gave me none, insisting that I stay with her. This surprised me, but I should have known better. As far as I can tell, Astri wouldn't know how to be rude if her life depended on it. She is tall and blond and the flight attendants on my flight could have been her sisters. She is gracious and sunny; she is the kind of person strangers say hello to on the street. Exactly the kind of person my father was not and exactly the kind of person I would like to be.

Astri and I met the first day of graduate school when I walked into class ten minutes early. She was standing on a chair in our rinky-dink writing classroom trying to open a window. Her lips were painted hot sauce red, and she was wearing the best of Alexis Bittar's latest jewelry collection. "Hello! I'm Astri. What's your name? Will you help me open this window? It's stuffy in here." She was right, of course, and what else could I do but hop on a neighboring chair and push?

I'm exhausted and a little nervous, too. I haven't seen Astri in months, and it is incredibly kind of her to let me stay with her, but it is almost somehow too kind. I am uncomfortable, because I am not sure I know how to accept this kindness. Though, of course, by coming, I have already accepted it.

Astri greets me with a hug, coffee, and fresh cardamom buns. She opens the glass doors that look out onto the street below, and we sit in the sun drinking our coffee and eating our buns. I forget why I was ever nervous or uncomfortable, and it occurs to me that if everyone made the sort of effort Astri does, the world would be a much happier place.

When we finish our *fika*, which means taking a break and usually involves drinking coffee or tea accompanied by something sweet, we go on a walk. In less than ten minutes I see both a fancy McDonald's beside a metro station and a calf, cappuccino brown, grazing in a field of tall grass. It's hard to believe I'm in the middle of a city with a population of more than one million.

In the afternoon, Astri has work to do. So do I. It seems appropriate to begin in Gamla Stan—the old city. After all, I am here because of the past; I am here to dig up the past. It's a leisurely twenty-minute walk to Gamla Stan from Astri's apartment, and I intend to take my time. It's late afternoon already when I finally set out, and the coffee and cardamom buns feel like a lifetime ago.

Swedish coffee is strong. Extremely strong. If you told me it was made not with water but with liquid meth, I would believe you. I feel slightly ill, and I have the shakes. My skin seems to have separated from my bones. Consuming the coffee on an empty, jet-lagged stomach didn't help. I can't even begin to imagine what America would be like if Starbucks sold Swedish coffee.

So I am shaking and happy and hungry. But still I take my time. My plan is to find a bit to eat in Gamla Stan and read the letters my father wrote from Stockholm. It had occurred to me to read them before I left New York. Make a list of the places he mentions. Look them up. Plan an itinerary. Arrive in Stockholm *prepared*.

But I told myself it would be more dramatic to wait. To read them where they had been written. Maybe I was just lazy. Or afraid. Afraid my dad would be boring. Afraid the letters would feel meaningless. Dull chatter. Pages and pages of weather reports and requests for money.

When my father lived here, Gamla Stan was still, officially anyway, Staden Mellan Broarna, which translates as "the town between the bridges" and refers to Stockholm's island geography. Gamla Stan is mostly just the island of Stadsholmen, although I learn that the smaller islands surrounding it—Riddarholmen, Helgeandsholmen, and Strömsborg—are also officially part of the old town as well. I walk slowly and carefully through the cobblestoned streets and narrow alleys, and I reject cafés: Too crowded. Overpriced. Smelly. Too touristy. Italian. I have a vision of reading these letters at an outside table drinking a Swedish beer and eating herring. But maybe I would have been better off going to the Ikea in Brooklyn. At last, I see a sign that says RESTAURANG with an arrow pointing down a narrow, half-hidden alley. Sold.

The herring is mediocre. The beer is decent. But the table is big and outside, the sun is shining but not oppressively so, and the letters are good.

I arrange them in chronological order, and I begin. It's August 25, 2011. On the thin sheets I'm holding, however, it's August 2, 1972, and my father is very much alive. In fact, he's so alive he's an asshole the way only a twenty-year-old can be. The first and last lines of his first letter home (as well as some lines in the middle) are about money. He wants to make sure his parents know how expensive Stockholm is. They should feel comfortable sending money. (This is the first of many moments when it occurs to me that not much has changed in thirty-nine years. I've been here less than a day, but it's already clear how expensive this city is.) There is something about recognizing my father as a young man—any young man, anywhere in time and place—that both reassures my heart and breaks it. That he was once just a kid is touching. But, also, oh god, he was just a kid. Just a kid.

His second letter also begins with money. He is, at least, consistent, and his needs are plain. Then he tells his parents that he is writing this letter from a pub in the old city. I don't know quite what to make of that, but it stops me. Stockholm's not exactly large, and people start pointing you in the direction of Gamla Stan even before you've left home; it's the first place everyone tells you to go. But neither his dorm nor the university were anywhere near Gamla Stan, and it's an area that lends itself more to drinking, eating, and shopping than sitting quietly to read or write. That my father wrote the letter in my hand in Gamla Stan and that I sit there now reading it for the first time—it's just a coincidence. I still don't believe things happen for a reason. But maybe every once in a while they end up that way. I put the letter in my lap, but gingerly because in their old age, the pages have begun to thin and wilt. I lay my palm over his words, and I look. I look at the cobblestone alley. I look at my beer, which I've barely touched, and the buildings rising around me, which, despite their age, look a lot stronger than anything in New York, where practically every other building is supported by scaffolding. He wrote these words here. Right here. And just like that, the shakes from the coffee stop. My bones and skin snap back together like magnets, and I am so glad I came.

For Christmas, he sent his father and mother individual cards, and it strikes me how hard he was trying to make them happy. I can relate. Each of their cards has a picture he's taken tucked inside. There are no people in the photos. To his mother, he sent a photograph taken in the forest behind his dorm. In the background, there's a row of trees lining the road. It must have been fall, because the trees are thick with leaves—leaves so yellow they look like gold-foil candy wrappers. There are so many leaves *on* the trees that it's surprising how many leaves are also *not* on the trees: the grass and road are paved in gold leaves. In the foreground is a lake. Two ducks swim away from the camera, disrupting the bright leaves floating in the water. It's not a lonely photo, but it is a solitary one. The road seems to stretch on forever, and I think of Dorothy on the yellow brick road on her way to see the wizard. Such a pretty road. You'd never guess how hard the trek. In his father's photo, fall has given way to winter. The trees are barren, devoid of both leaves and, strangely, branches, so that they look like sickly sticks stuck in the ground and abandoned. Patches of snow hide the ground, and the lake is frozen. Just looking at the photo makes me cold. *God jul och gott nytt år.*

I FIND MY father's Stockholm address on the back of his letters. He sent aerograms; letters that are sent via airmail and are made out of the thinnest writing paper, which you fold up to make an envelope. Because the post office knows exactly how much each aerogram weighs and because you can't add any additional pages or your own envelope, the postage is predetermined and they come with an imprinted stamp already in place. This is just the kind of thing my father loved: logical and efficient. A small invention that makes all the difference.

The address isn't far from Astri's apartment, and I take the metro. But it's not the city, either, and when I get off the train and take the escalator up to the street, I find myself in what can only be described as the country. It's green and lush with trees that go up and up and up. But instead of suburban homes peeking out from behind the tree trunks, I find apartment buildings. Dorms, mostly, I realize. I've stumbled upon some sort of student housing commune. Everyone looks twenty years old, and they carry backpacks or six-packs or both. It's Friday afternoon, and they're preparing for the weekend ahead.

My father's address is tricky because it gives neither a street nor any discernible address number. I learn later that the "Kungshamra," which makes up practically the whole of the address, is the name of the student housing community my father lived in. This community encompasses several blocks of buildings. It's a bit like if my address were simply West Village NYC. But I don't know this; I don't know enough to be discouraged. When I plug the address into Google Maps, Google, miraculously, gives me directions to a street, albeit a street not mentioned in any part of my father's address. I follow Google's directions, because what other options do I have? The trouble starts when I reach my destination. I've arrived, according to Google. I see nothing that says Kungshamra. I still don't realize that isn't what I'm looking for. Nor do I see any of the ten numbers that follow Kungshamra in my father's address. All I see is one long block of concrete apartment complexes surrounded by woods. This is the forest my father wrote about. My father mentions jogging in the forest in his letters home. The pictures he sent at Christmas to his parents are from "the forest." What was unclear from his letters and his photographs, though, is how much this street and these woods remind me of my father's neighborhood and condo in Santa Cruz, California.

It's the same clean dirt scent. Piney, salty, crispy. Water is somewhere nearby, and you can smell it. Feel it, too, cool on the skin. In Santa Cruz, I am always struck with the sensation that what I smell and the way the air feels against my skin is much the same as what the Spanish settlers must have smelt and felt when they stumbled upon the area in the 1700s. The same cannot be said of New York City, or, for that matter, much of Stockholm, I imagine. But here, in the suburbs of the Swedish city, everything feels untouched, as though it's been preserved for thirty-nine years. Just waiting for me. This must be the place.

I sit down on the curb, because I don't know which building was my father's, and I think, what I see right now, he saw. What I smell right now, he smelt. What I feel, he felt. And he must have liked it, because he found himself the Northern California version twenty years later. His condo in Santa Cruz was a two-story box. Modern and efficient. The windows were long and rectangular, much like the Stockholm dorm windows above me now. At the end of his block was a patch of redwoods and a little path that led to a park, with stairs leading down to a hot-dog shack and a public beach. He never brought up Stockholm in the context of Santa Cruz, and I wonder if he ever made the connection. It occurs to me that I may be the only person in my father's life who has seen both his Stockholm home and his Santa Cruz home. The only person alive who could possibly make that connection. Except, of course, for the ever-elusive Daniel, who managed to answer all of my questions and yet reveal almost nothing . . . just like my father. Daniel said he hadn't seen much of my father when he lived in Santa Cruz, but, who knows, maybe once or twice he did visit my dad's condo. I have no idea, and I probably never will. Thinking about Daniel makes me feel worse than I already do. I must be *so close* to my father's dorm, and yet, it eludes me.

Then I see the vomit in the gutter, mere inches from my feet. It is still early Friday, but the students of Stockholm University are apparently wasting no time. I stand, and when I do, I notice a small white tile nailed to the side of one of the dorms. On it is the number seventy-one. The ten-digit number in my father's address includes a seven and a one next to each other, and upon closer inspection, they might actually stand alone from the remaining eight numbers. My hypothesis may be flimsy, but it's as good a guess as any. It beats sitting in the gutter with vomit, and what if I'm right? I feel light-headed and the whole world has gone slow. One of those moments when you feel outside of yourself, like you're watching the Lifetime movie of your life.

I walk around the side to the interior courtyard and what looks like the entrance to building number seventy-one. The heavy black doors are locked. But I can see a staircase and a row of mailboxes and a long hallway lined with doors, presumably leading to student rooms. It's just a lousy dorm. Someone says something in Swedish behind me, and I turn around to see a young man leaning out a window on the first floor. He's holding a stick of butter, and I take this as a good sign. Butter isn't very threatening. He is pale with dark brown hair and dark eyes. We could be siblings. I ask him if he speaks English, and he says, "Yeah, yeah." I show him my father's address. "Am I here?"

He laughs at me and smiles. "Yeah, yeah." Then he disappears. He reappears on the other side of the heavy black door and holds it open for me. He's still holding the stick of butter.

"You have a friend here?" I shake my head no. Not exactly. But before I can explain, he points to a mailbox with more of the numbers from my father's address. "This is the mailbox you have," he says as he looks down at the address in my hand. My father's mailbox. This is where he got the answers to all his letters. "You want to see the room, too?" I nod. "It's here on my floor," he says, as he leads me down the hallway. We stop in front of a door, and my new friend bangs on it. We wait in silence. He bangs again. Nothing. "Your friend isn't home."

I shake my head. "It's not my friend. My dad, uh, lived here in the seventies."

He looks confused. "In the seventies?"

I'm not sure if he simply finds my mission odd or if he doesn't understand what I mean by "the seventies" or both.

"My dad lived here a long time ago. As a student."

"I can't get in," the boy replies. He seems very sorry.

"It's okay," I tell him. "Thank you."

We start to walk back down the hallway. I imagine his butter must be starting to melt in his hand.

"Where do you live?"

"I live in New York."

He breaks out into a grin.

"Oh! New York!" He waves his hands—the butter—in the air and says, "Fancy!"

I laugh.

But then his features cloud.

"But you are French?"

The question comes apropos of nothing. I think of my last name and the distant relatives I have scattered around France and whom I have never met.

"Well, sort of."

He looks confused again.

"I mean, yes. By blood."

Now he looks really confused.

"But I have never been to France."

He seems to understand. Or, rather, he nods.

"French, but you've never been to France?"

He poses it as a question, but I have no answer. And I think, Jesus, what is it about me when I travel abroad that strange men end up beseeching me to go to France. I feel obligated to respond. To somehow reassure him so he doesn't look so disappointed.

"But I'm going! That's where I'm headed. To France, I mean. I'm going to Paris. From here. I'm flying there." I can't seem to shut up.

We reach the heavy black doors again, and I thank him again, and stick out my hand to shake. He offers his hand with the butter and laughs as he shoves the butter in his pocket before offering me his hand again. We shake, and I learn I was right; the butter was melting in his hand. He lets me out, and I hear the door shut behind me. I stand still for a moment. Friend, whose name I just now realize I never got, is standing back in his kitchen window. And we're right back where we started ten minutes ago, only now I know I am here. I am at my father's old home. I found it. Hand smeared by butter. One less piece of him missing. I think of the few photos I have seen of him from this time. He wore his hair long here. I see him walking up the dorm steps, arms full of books. I see him reclining, because he was a recliner, not a sitter, on a bench in the courtyard talking with Frederick, maybe. He lived here. He was happy here. I can't really know if that's true or not, but I choose to believe that it is. That's enough.

WALKING BACK TOWARD the street, I realize that I'm passing a window at the other end of my father's hallway. I peer in. I see his door and beyond it, tiny now, the mailboxes. The window is clean, and I can see everything inside clearly, so I turn off the flash on my camera and take two pictures. I snap several more of the courtyard and the outside of the building. Later, when I upload the photos to my computer, every one turns out sharp and predictably unremarkable. All of them except for the two of the hallway. Both of which are clear where my father's door is but foggy everywhere else; there is a well-defined ring around my father's door in each photo, but the rest of the shot is smoky. Not blurry. Just smoky. Like a layer of fog has been applied to the entire photo except for my father's door. It's like someone has turned a spotlight on my father's door.

At the end of my father's block I find a yellow piece of paper torn from a legal pad. On it, someone has written "Metro Stop Bershamra, 71 Kungshamra" in blue ink: the metro stop I took to get here and my father's building. This isn't earth-shattering. I know that. But it makes me feel as though there's something looking out for me. That something wanted to make sure I found what I came looking for. And I have. But have I found what I needed to find?

This scrap of paper is on the ground in front of a fast-food shack, the only business on the otherwise residential block. When I arrived, I paid very little attention to it; I doubt it was around when my father lived here. But I notice now that it's Benny's Pizza Bar and Grill and that it offers student dis-counts and "take away" deals. And even though, or perhaps because, Ben hates the nickname Benny, it makes me think of him. It seems only fitting that he should pop up now in the form of a greasy burger joint with a single window for ordering and picking up and two outdoor picnic tables for eating. It's a Ben kind of place. Dirty and run-down, Benny's doesn't care what you think. I don't stop though. I have dinner plans. Plans that Ben would scoff at, but he's not here, and I am.

BEN IS IN Brooklyn. He lives in Carroll Gardens—so named for Charles Carroll, the only Catholic who signed the Declaration of Independence. The neighborhood has strong Italian-Catholic roots, and elderly Italian housewives still sit on the sidewalk in folding chairs, the aprons around their thick waists yellowed with age. They have front-row seats to gentrification, and they do not hesitate to hiss at a young woman walking by in a short short skirt. The kind of skirt the nuns never would have let her get away with in grammar school. Trust me, I know. The Dunkin' Donuts on the corner of Ben's block has a courtyard attached with a statue of Jesus, so even if you don't go to church on Sunday you still get a little bit of God with your coffee and your Old-Fashioned donut. Even Al Capone himself got married at the beautiful St. Mary's Catholic Church on Court Street. It's a fabulous hood.

The wedding Ben has invited me to is in another of my favorite Brooklyn neighborhoods. Greenpoint borders the East River and has a rich shipbuilding history and a large Polish population dating back to the mid-nineteenth century. Ben and I agree to meet at a bar that, supposedly, once catered to dockworkers. The weather has been moody all day: windy and either raining or drizzling in such a fashion that a downpour feels constantly imminent. Greenpoint, with its one fickle subway line, is not the most convenient of neighborhoods to reach. It has its own thing going on. I suspect it's a point of pride for its residents that it's so hard to get there. Only the weak need multiple and reliable subway lines.

But I get there. Early, even, because I overcompensate for the rain. In what will become something of a pattern between us, I arrive before Ben. I sit on a bar stool in my silk dress and heels, and I can picture the dockworkers piling in after a long shift. The wide planks of the wooden floors are different lengths and widths and come in every shade of worn. Behind the bar is the quintessential exposed brick and there's even an apothecary cabinet. But the bartender is a woman in jeans, and after placing my drink in front of me, she lets me alone. Ben and I text. He's coming. He's only ten minutes away. I suspect that ten minutes more likely means a substantially higher multiple of ten. But I don't care. I am happy for the time alone. Sometimes, the most perfect thing is just to sit at the bar all dressed up nursing a cocktail watching everyone else make connections.

I am grateful to Ben's friends for so generously inviting me to their wedding; they didn't invite Ben with a guest, but Ben had told the groom about me and William and his guilt and his confusion, and the groom had said to him, "Look, you really like this girl. Bring her to the wedding." William and I haven't had any contact in months, and I adore Ben, but the situation doesn't feel good. Then Ben, twenty minutes late, strolls into the bar, and I remind myself that we're supposed to be just friends tonight.

The ceremony is held at Congregation Ahavas Israel, a 120-year-old synagogue. Greenpoint once supported five synagogues but only Ahavas Israel remains. It is a beautiful synagogue, and it feels like being in a well-loved home, which I suppose it is. We sit on dark wood benches that someone waxed until they shone, and the candle sconces on the walls flicker above our heads. Every seat is occupied and we sit squished, but it is a small synagogue and the intimacy feels exactly right. Two aisles separate the rows of benches, and the bride and groom enter simultaneously; the groom walks up one aisle with his parents, and the bride walks up the other with hers. All six of them are grinning.

When they reach the rabbi, the bride and groom hug their parents before turning away to stand together beneath the chuppah. But the rabbi asks them to turn back. He tells them to look at each other and now look out at us—their family, friends, and guests. He asks them to consider the moment. To be fully present in their wedding ceremony, to feel where they are, who they are with, and why they are here. And they do. They look at each other. They look at us. We look back at them. I have never met these people. Ben and the groom have known each other since high school, but I first laid eyes on them as they walked up the aisle to be married. The only person I know here is Ben. But, somehow, in this moment sitting close to Ben in an old synagogue celebrating an ancient religion that bears little resemblance to the Catholicism I grew up with, I am so grateful to be here, to support this couple in their wedding and their marriage to come. I have attended trendy weddings where the ceremony feels almost like an afterthought—those weddings are all about the reception, the party and the favors that match the invitations and the fondant on the cake. This is one of the first weddings I've been to that feels like the beginning of a marriage and not just a blowout prom.

I wonder, not for the first time, about my parents' wedding. I have never seen an album—just an orange-and-brown shoebox full of proofs. It did happen. My mother in a long-sleeved gown she designed herself, her hair parted down the middle and flat against her back. The morning of the ceremony she made herself a crown of roses. No veil. Each of her bridesmaids carried a single red rose. No florist. After, they had dinner at a cloth-napkin restaurant on a cobblestoned street near the Sacramento River. No dancing. That wedding, too, was the beginning of something. Not the marriage it should have been, but the kind of friendship people spend their whole lives searching for.

The rabbi invites the bride's and groom's grandparents, parents, and a few of their other married friends and family to come up and speak about marriage, love, and relationships. They come forward and encircle the bride and groom. Their grandparents have been married for decades, while some of their friends are newlyweds. But all of these married couples have something to share and have prepared their thoughts on index cards and sheets of notebook paper. They speak about what marriage means to them, what it has taught them, what they love about it, what they hate about it, what makes it easy, and what they wish they had known on their wedding day.

I get it. This is why couples get married and have weddings. Because it isn't just about *not* breaking up and sharing an address. This bride and groom are choosing to build a life together, and they are asking their community to support and encourage their decision today and in all the years to come. It's huge and powerful. I think about the people I know who have gotten married; most of them remember little of their wedding day. *It went by in a blur.* Watching Ben's friends say their vows and exchange their rings, that seems especially sad to me now. Shouldn't this moment, of all the moments, be long and firmly rooted in your memory of experiences? Because marriage is long, and it seems to me that there are many times when couples doubt themselves and their spouses and their reasons for being together. On those occasions, I imagine it might help to be able to think back on your wedding ceremony and everyone who was there and that moment you said, "I do," and really meant it and really believed you could, do. Maybe that's the secret: you don't *need* your wedding on your wedding day. You need your wedding and the memory of it and the legality of it later when you face the trials and struggles of a marriage.

The reception is a few blocks away at a banquet hall, and so we walk. It's not raining, but it must have rained heavily during the ceremony because the streets are dark and wet and cool. Clean.

Ben and I have, so far, maintained our friendship pact. We walk close but not too close. He doesn't reach for my hand or put his arm around me. We haven't touched. Yet, even just walking beside him feels intimate. We have rhythm.

At the reception, our table is the farthest away from the stage and the closest to the bar. But I don't drink and Ben hardly touches his scotch. This is our second pact, I suppose. An unacknowledged mutual understanding. Not that it matters. Because we're at our table in back, tucked into a corner, largely forgotten and sober, when we break our pacts. The master of ceremonies makes a joke, and I lean forward to whisper something about it in Ben's ear. As I do, he puts his hand on the small of my back. That's all it takes. I feel the heat and the slight pressure of his palm through my dress, and I know we aren't friends anymore.

The next morning we woke up in Ben's bed in an extremely friendly position. I'd been in similar situations before but never without a massive hangover. This was also the first time I wanted to stay. It was early, ish. But what had woken us was Ben's phone. The groom was calling, which struck both Ben and me as peculiar. There are very few people you might call in the morning on your first day as a married man, and although I knew Ben and the groom were close, they weren't that close. Ben let it go to voice mail. Eventually, though, he did call his friend, who only wanted to report an amusing anecdote from the tail end of the reception. Apparently, while Ben and I were on the dance floor, the groom's mother asked him if Ben and his lady friend were demonstrating, what was it called, freaking?

We hadn't spoken to this woman once the night before, and yet, it had been obvious to her that we were together. We were together. But we couldn't do everything together. I still had to find my dad on my own. Ben couldn't fix my past for me, and I didn't want him to.

16

IN THE LETTERS MY FATHER WROTE FROM SWE-
den, he talks about the food he ate. The escargot in both
Stockholm and Paris. The pastries. The Christmas wine. The
pheasant. The chocolate. Becoming a parent didn't change his
approach to food. While my friends' parents served them
buttered pasta and crustless bread, my father fed me cow
tongue. We were at Noriega's, a Basque restaurant in Bakersfield, sitting on benches at a long picnic-style table. He was
sitting next to me, and he put the meat on my plate. "Eat this,"
he said. I asked him what it was. "Just try it." I was suspicious.
But I tried it. I remember nothing of what it tasted like, only
that it wasn't bad. But I do remember his face. "Do you like
it?" I nodded and asked again what I was eating. He spoke
slowly, and his eyes twinkled. "It's tongue. Cow tongue." I
gagged. He waggled his finger at me. "You already said you
liked it!"

He taught me well. At brunch one Sunday we went to a
new restaurant. I was in first grade. It's a Mexican restaurant
now, but then it was an American bistro and one of the first
restaurants in Sacramento to emphasize the use of fresh and
local ingredients. I asked the waiter if he recommended the
oatmeal or the frittata. He found this hilarious and told me

they were both good, which was not helpful and annoyed me. I ordered the oatmeal. After our food had come, the waiter asked me how I liked my oatmeal. I told him it was divine. I don't think my father ever looked more pleased with me than he did in that moment.

If I am in Stockholm for my father, then I must eat like it. I did my research. Bon Bon is the place. But the restaurant is farther away than I anticipate, and my long walk there takes me down dark, quiet streets the likes of which are rare in Manhattan, where most everything is lit up and flashing, alarming. At first I relish the stillness; walking through Stockholm after dark—and this goes for most European cities I've been to—feels a bit like walking through a painting of an ancient city at night. Everything is beautiful and nothing moves. The shops are closed, and the people are inside. So, if you are out, the city is all yours. It all belongs to you—the wide streets, the lampposts, the trees and the water, even the bicycles chained to themselves alongside your buildings. So much real estate to call your own.

But soon the darkness and the silence start to feel minatory. I stop meandering and that signature tourist grin goes slack. I pick up my pace and check behind me every few feet. I am alone. Too alone. So it is that by the time I finally spot the honey-colored light of Bon Bon's dining room, I am not only hungry but also grateful, which, as a former hostess, waitress, and bartender, I happen to know is the ideal customer state of mind.

Four exquisite Swedish women do everything but cook at Bon Bon. They wear matching floral minidresses and black sneakers, and the loudest thing about them is their smiles. I don't have a reservation, and they're slammed. But I am a party of one, and they graciously tuck me into the far corner of the bar, and it is perfect. The cocktail and wine list is, naturally, in Swedish, but sparkling wine is universal, and my glass of cava appears almost before I've finished requesting it: I watch the tiniest stream of bubbles jet toward the surface like fireworks shooting across the sky just before they go off.

I think of Daniel's words: *Lou loved wine.*

There is bread and the kind of olive oil that stands on its own: it tastes like grassy roasted almonds, if there is such a thing. I imagine almonds rolling down a grassy hill. I can hear my father saying, *This is how you taste, Victoria. Slowly now. Don't eat. Taste.* Eating is for hungry people. Tasting is for the lucky. We are lucky.

At Bon Bon, patrons order drinks and dessert. But everything in between is brought out on oversized circular trays and presented tableside by the women. The courses are small, tapas style, and patrons are invited to choose, round by round, if they want to try that course. Every time you say yes, a marble is dropped in a small vase on your table. At the end of the night, the women count your marbles; the more marbles you have in your vase, the more you owe. It amazes me that the marbles are kept on your table. Surely, patrons sometimes "accidentally" lose their marbles when no one is looking?

I accrue five marbles (no cheating):

+ Steak tartare with caviar and mollified egg yolk on a bed of buttered toast, and the secret is the buttered toast. The juices and softness of the meat, the fish, and the yolk seep into the crispy bread and melted butter. Comfort food.
+ Escargot with garlic, butter, and pesto: the two snails are warm stopping just short of hot, and they are served on fat salt crystals that shatter under my teeth. I hold the shells upside down over my spoon and let the butter, garlic, and pesto pool. I discard the empty shells, pale with sandy stripes, on the beach of salt. And though they are

empty of meat and sauce, I am sad to see the pretty shells go when the waitress whisks them away.

+ Brisket with red wine sauce, pickled chanterelle mushrooms, and mashed potatoes with chives. *This is how you taste, Victoria.* The effort of the pickling feels a waste; I taste only red-wine beef and potatoes.

+ A scallop with caviar and oyster sauce and ribbons of cucumber served in an open shell. It tastes like the sea and reminds me of the first time I tried wake boarding. I was with my father, and I went under with a wave. I couldn't tell which way was up and which way was down. I swallowed the ocean with my eyes, my nose, and my mouth; thick ocean water coated my eyes, nostrils, and mouth, and I was pickled. When I finally broke the surface, he was right there. Right beside me all along. Watching me. Waiting for me. He smiled. He didn't seem to understand my fear. I hadn't known he was there, and because I hadn't known, because I had felt alone and helpless, did his presence count?

+ Pike fish, carrot puree (baby food really), and toothpick-sized sweet potato fries served atop a cool lemon cream sauce. The sweet potato fries and the carrot puree are cloyingly sweet, but the pike is silky and the pepper flakes tucked beneath its skin take me by surprise. And there is one bite with fish, pepper, and lemon, slippery in mouth, that I think, *Aw, here is the chef's vision. This is what he was thinking.*

There is such a thing as the perfect bite, and it has nothing to do with what you are eating. It's the *how.* I use my knife and fork to cut, pile, and construct a pyramid layering each of the flavors of a dish in my spoon; now, I slurp that bite right out of the spoon's belly. *This is how you taste.*

I say no to dessert, but I don't leave. I remain in my corner, eyeing the liquor bottles behind the bar, each of which has a pretty label. Everything here—liquor, food, the waitresses' shoes, the wobbly wooden chairs—feels like haphazard glamour. This restaurant and every restaurant, every bar, every hotel is trying to be the prettiest girl at the party. All of it reminds me of my father. Elegance, opulence, they made him feel safe. *Ninety percent of anything is presentation, Victoria.*

These restaurants with their tiny foods and candlelight and fancy liquor bottle labels: they feel as if they have been my whole life. I think of all the restaurants William and I went to. The long meals with tablecloths and multiple forks and cocktails we shared on Tuesday nights just because. All I ever did was taste. Food. Men. It would have been nice to just eat sometimes. Like at Benny's Pizza Bar and Grill. I could have. I can't blame William or any of the other men I dined with. I'm the one who billed myself as a sophisticated connoisseur of amuse bouche. I'm the one who was 90 percent presentation.

One of the exquisite women in floral is standing in front of the open beer refrigerator. She leans back against the cold glass bottles, and they knock together. This is happening behind the bar. Right in front of me. I see the look on her face as the cool air hits the back of her neck and thighs. Relief. She smiles at me. I smile back. In her little dress, surrounded by all that beer, she looks like she belongs at a barbecue. A beautiful barbecue. I ask her which one is her favorite. She points to a bottle on the bottom shelf near her foot. I order it.

Another exquisite woman makes a dessert cocktail in front of me. Some sort of lemon meringue martini by the looks of it. I want nothing to do with it, but then she peels a long ribbon lemon rind, and the scent is so strong and so sparkling that it makes everything sharp. My cava fog, my food coma— they evaporate. That's when I realize that I am alone.

The restaurant has cleared out. The lemon meringue martini is for the one table still occupied. Another exquisite woman counts my marbles and asks which dish was my favorite. I open my mouth to answer, but suddenly I cannot remember any of them. Not one. The correct answer is the escargot. But I won't remember those two snails until later when I look at my notes. How could I forget so quickly? After all that slow chewing and thoughtfulness and tasting and note-taking, I remember nothing.

My walk home from Bon Bon felt much shorter. But of course now I had two glasses of cava and a beer in me, and I was admittedly tipsy. I wasn't drinking as much as I used to and my tolerance had become a joke. I felt tall and was very aware of my legs. They were carrying me home like magic. I was gliding on this sidewalk under these Swedish trees! The number of times I have walked home alone drunk and vulnerable is higher than I care to admit. I have no idea what that number might actually be; however, there is little doubt it's stupidly high. But once more I made it home entirely intact and was amazed to learn it was after two A.M. I fell asleep immediately. In the morning, I was pleased with myself for having drunk just enough to sleep the solid, satisfying sleep of drink but not so much that I had a hangover.

But my buoyance and health are short-lived. I eat herring for lunch at an obnoxiously trendy and overpriced café in the center of Stockholm that everyone recommends. An hour later I can't stand up straight, the cramps in my stomach are so bad. My breathing is limited to short, rapid puffs. Twenty minutes later I lock myself in the bathroom of the Stockholm Public Library and shit my brains out. I am desecrating my favorite place in Stockholm. Only I don't know that yet. When I finally peel myself off the toilet, I pull myself together, and walk back outside, determined to have another look at the library's exterior. I am here because I love libraries. You can tell a lot about a city and its people based on how they take care of their books. Everyone in Stockholm had told me I should come here. They were proud of their library, and that was a wonderful sign. I am also here because renowned Swedish architect Gunnar Asplund designed it. He finished it in 1928, and it's considered one of his most significant designs and a prominent building in Stockholm. My father didn't mention the library in any of the letters I have, but it is inconceivable to me that he was never here.

The Stockholm Public Library is a beautiful building. A cylinder sits on the roof like a cake topper. The whole thing is painted a single shade of red dirt, and it glows in the sun as I walk up a gently sloping ramp to the large glass entrance. Inside, curved shelves have been built around the main rotunda and a glass bowl chandelier hangs in the center. It is like stepping into an arena of books. A maze of smaller rooms adjoins the rotunda, and many of them are as intimate as the rotunda is grand. Tucked into corners and placed on windowsills are vases of fresh flowers. Later, I will remember most vividly the light. It was the sunniest library I had ever been in. A library for social people.

I am told the architect was inspired by the Rotunda of the Villette in Paris, but his design is considered an example of Nordic Classicism, a style that combined elements of Neoclassicism with Modernism. Old and young. His lines are far less fussy than in Paris's Rotunda. Walking both around the library and through, I imagine Gunnar as a potter bent over coils of clay, shaping them into smooth, unadorned forms. I see my father's kitchen remodel in Gunnar's lines. Nordic Classicism is sometimes called Swedish Grace, and that's exactly what the library is. A place of grace.

I leave reluctantly and just when I've walked too far to turn back and use the library's restroom, I am hit with a second bout of violent diarrhea. I pay some ungodly amount of Swedish kroner to use a disgusting McDonald's bathroom, which I proceed to make more disgusting. I am sweating profusely. I should go home. But I don't. I have a dinner reservation at a Michelin star restaurant, Rolf's Kok, and I am determined not to miss it. I spend the rest of the afternoon moving from public restroom to public restroom—coffee shops, another McDonald's, a mall, a bar, a hotel lobby—until it is time for my dinner reservation. I know this is ludicrous. Sweating, cramping, an inability to stand up straight, the aforementioned shitting. None of it goes away. In fact, it gets worse. But for some reason I can't accept that it's not going away. I've never experienced anything like this before, and it seems to me that it's always just about to end. But it doesn't.

I take a table near the bathroom of Rolf's. I order the escargot and the seafood pasta. Rolls arrive not in a basket but stacked on what looks like a giant needle. They are warm and fluffy and practically fall apart in your hands as you take them off the needle, one by one. But I can eat barely half of one. I go to the bathroom, and while I am washing my hands, I realize I need to get back on the toilet. I wash my hands two more times. When I limp back to my table, my snails greet me. These I manage to eat. They have a tomato-and-garlic-based sauce and as they slide down my throat I am conscious, somewhere in my brain, that they are very good. If only I could enjoy them.

I cannot eat my pasta, but I suspect it of being delicious.

I go to the bathroom again.

The waitress asks if I would like dessert. I have an out-of-body experience in which I see and hear myself say, "I'll have the King Oscar Cake." I cannot wholly believe this is actually me or that I am actually saying these words. I never order the cake on dessert menus. I don't like cake. I am a tart-pie-crumble kind of girl. I am crumbling. I know that what I have just ordered I would not like on my best day. Today is not my best day.

I go to the bathroom.

When I come out, the waitress asks if I am okay. She looks genuinely concerned, which I find reassuring as it means she doesn't think I'm a cokehead. My cake arrives. There are layers of baked meringue, which are crunchy, and layers of white frosting. It is an enormous slice of sugar. I am sure it is an exceptional example of King Oscar Cake, but I hate it. The waitress keeps sneaking glances at me. I keep eating. I am trying very hard not to taste it. Suddenly it's gone, and I feel worse than I have all day. I pay. I tip absurdly. I go to the bathroom again. Then I get stupider.

I walk home. I pretend I'm going to take the first cab I see, but I don't want to spend the money. I hate spending money on transportation. It feels like shredding money. I will drop thirty dollars on snails without a second thought, but I will hate myself for days if I take a cab. I walk. I stop in two bars to use the bathroom, and I have to kneel at least twice on every block because the cramping is so bad I am dizzy and cannot stand up straight.

When I finally reach my friend's apartment, I thank god she is spending the weekend at her parents' home outside the city. I eat a spoonful of yogurt and half a miniature banana, because even though the notion of more food horrifies me, the Internet tells me these will help. I try to lie down, but I am getting up and crawling to the bathroom so often that I finally give up and just lie down on the bathroom floor. I try not to think about how much of my friend's toilet paper I am using. I am butchering entire Swedish forests. And I am crying. A lot. I am crying and cursing the herring and the King Oscar Cake, but still I am happy to be so near a toilet and one with such a cool porcelain base to rest my head against.

*   *   *

ABOUT A YEAR before my father's death, shortly before he was bedridden, he fell. It was in the night. We were alone in his house, he in his room and me in mine. He had gotten up to get a glass of water. Walking back to his room and carrying the glass in one hand, his legs crumpled. It happened in the living room. He fell silently, unwavering in his refusal to acknowledge pain or need; it was the shattering of the glass on the hardwood floor that woke me. I found him leaning against the back of the couch, his cheek pressed into the leather. His breath was labored and his face red. The cool water wet the bottoms of my bare toes, and I saw the broken shards of glass as my father saw me.

"Don't. Don't step any closer," he said, his voice strained but firm.

I didn't move.

"Go back to bed."

"But," I started to reply.

"Go."

Something in his voice told me not to disobey.

In bed, I lay awake on top of the covers. For a long time the house was quiet. The shadow of a branch from the tree outside my window fell on the wall. I'd spent many afternoons in that tree reading and watching the neighborhood. It didn't look nearly so inviting in the middle of the night. Eventually, when he could muster the strength, my father shuffled by my door and into his bedroom across the hall. I waited until I was confident he was asleep. I put on my slippers and took the long way to the kitchen. I moved slowly, afraid I would get caught. I brought the roll of paper towels to the living room, and, guided by the moonlight streaming in between the slats in the shutters, wiped away the water and the shimmery bits of glass. I threw away the wet paper towels studded with glass and returned to my room.

In the morning, my father asked how I had slept. I said fine, and he agreed that he had also slept fine. I didn't mention the fresh bruise on his arm.

WHEN ASTRI COMES home from her parents' house on Sunday night, I decamp to a hotel, too embarrassed to stay. I knew she had a busy workweek ahead, and I didn't want to bother her with my sick-making. It's one thing to accept a friend's gracious hospitality for a week or two. It is quite another to put a friend in the proximity of your strenuous bowel movements.

At last, I stop sweating quite so much and the cramping mostly subsides and I convince myself I am feeling better. I need air. I walk toward the water. Patti Smith's face is all over the city on banners hanging from streetlamps and on posters underground lining the walls of the metro stations. She's being honored as a Polar Music Prize Laureate at the Stockholm Concert Hall, and the ceremony is in Stockholm on the day I am scheduled to leave. But I haven't left yet, and it feels as though she's walking alongside me.

The photograph on the poster is Patti Smith at her most Patti Smith: Black suit. Black hat. Long dark hair framing her long pale face. Hands raised to her chest. Palms in. Long fingers touching. She looks almost as though she's in prayer. Like she's praying for everyone who walks beneath her image. The corners of her mouth turn ever so slightly down and it would be easy to think she's frowning. But the corners of my mother's mouth do that, too, and it's not a frown. It's just the way their lips settle.

By an odd coincidence, there is a Robert Mapplethorpe exhibit at Stockholm's Fotografiska. Mapplethorpe died of complications of AIDS in March 1989. Two months later my father tested positive for HIV, and so began the end of his life. I find myself walking along the water in the direction of the museum, and it feels like Patti Smith is guiding my exhausted, sick, sore self there. Maybe she is.

The exhibit includes nearly two hundred of his photographs, including, of course, his iconic flowers. But the flowers feel almost like an afterthought. There are far more of his nudes, his S&M portraits, and his friends and their children. Patti Smith is everywhere—as a wife and mother and earlier as an artist, a muse, and in the beginning as a girl-woman in the seventies, uncertain. The exhibit is crowded, but I get up close to these images until my nose is nearly pressed against the glass. Her lips droop down in even the earliest shots, and I think of my mother and her mouth.

She told me once that sometimes, especially when she was younger, strangers on the street would mistake her for frowning and admonish her: "Smile! It's a beautiful day." I wonder if that's ever happened to Patti.

All of the Patti photographs predate the image of her plastered all over the city outside this museum. It's like I woke up this morning with the Patti Smith of today, and now I'm traveling backward through her life. I look at these images taken in the eighties and the seventies, and I know things she doesn't know. I read my father's letters, and I stand outside his apartment in Stockholm, and I know things he didn't know when he shut that door for the last time and flew home to California. Mapplethorpe's photos are meticulous. Sharp. Sometimes, for a moment, looking at one, I think it's a sad photo. But maybe it's not. Maybe the edges—the corners—of the image just turn down naturally, not in sadness but just as fact. Neither sad nor happy. I don't linger at the exhibit because it turns out I'm not done being sick. I half-crawl back to my hotel room and spend my last night in Stockholm in the bathroom.

I don't want to leave. Stockholm was supposed to be for my father, and Paris was supposed to be for me. But I have fallen in love with this city. Unlike New York, Stockholm never forgets it was built on islands. The water is fully present. But so are the trees. It's urban and rural, neither diminished. Color! The Swedish textiles are whimsical without being unsophisticated. Bright striped patterns of yellows, reds, blues, and greens and swirling floral prints in purples, golds, and ruby reds. I love that instead of heat lamps, outdoor bars and restaurants have piles of thick blankets stashed in corners; grab one when you need it. I love the cardamom buns and the coffee that is not messing around. It's like the Swedes just do life better than the rest of us. Is this how my dad felt?

But I have to go. It's time to fly to Paris on the airline that advertises itself, with pride, as the cheapest European planes. I'm still sick. I spend twenty minutes trapped inside the airplane bathroom before the captain turns on the seat belt sign, and I timidly return to my seat. We land, and a funny thing happens: I'm cured. Whatever it was, I leave it on the plane and send it back to Sweden.

17

A T FIRST, BEN AND I GO BACK AND FORTH BE-
tween his apartment in Brooklyn and mine in Manhattan. But schlepping back and forth is a hassle—as any couple
living separately, but especially in New York City, can attest.
Whatever you need is always at the other apartment: face
wash, clean underwear, that one belt, cell phone charger. The
schlepping bothers me more than it bothers Ben. Mostly, I
suspect, because he doesn't wash his face or care about clean
underwear. And though his cell phone battery dies almost
daily, he is never in any hurry to charge it.

There is also the issue of his bathroom. Ben has a daily
yoga practice and usually showers after class in the studio
locker room. Since he rarely washes his face, his bathroom sees
very little action. For Ben's purposes, his bathroom is entirely
sufficient. For my purposes, his bathroom is traumatizing.

It's bad enough that the bathroom hasn't been cleaned
since Ben's ex-girlfriend moved out two years before I ever
laid eyes on it, but the sink is the size and depth of a dinner
plate. When I wash my face using this pathetic sink, so
much water spills everywhere that I might as well be washing my feet. There is also no counter, which means no counter space. Once, after attempting to go to the bathroom

without touching anything, I flushed the toilet and turned to wash my hands. In doing so, I knocked a bottle of lotion into the toilet bowl, and it disappeared with the final flush.

The toilet is average size and is sandwiched between the dollhouse sink and the tub/shower monstrosity. I have to climb over the toilet to get in and out of the shower. And once in the shower, it's still no picnic. Sometimes the water is hot. Sometimes the water is cold. Always the tub is dirty. There's also a mysterious caulking situation where the tub and tile meet. Someone caulked the hell out of that tub. The caulking, which has dried beige, is several inches tall and several inches wide and makes it seem as though some sort of foreboding oozy mass is seeping out of the tile and into the tub. Ben claims the caulking incident occurred near the end of his relationship with his ex. He was on a trip, and they were fighting long distance. At some point, she took her anger out on the tub.

This is surely an incomplete explanation, but relationships are messy, and anger, pain, and frustration can drive us all to do bizarre things. I'm in no position to judge other people. But I am more than happy to judge things and places and spaces, and I hate Ben's bathroom. Which is why, when we discuss the possibility of moving in together, I am adamant that his bathroom never becomes our bathroom. So, this being New York City, where finding shelter is always a nightmare, Ben moves into my apartment.

Yes, I blame the bathroom. I blame the ghost of the ex-girlfriend, too. I didn't want to move into an apartment that Ben had shared with another woman. But it wasn't just that. Some things in life are more important than toilets and has-been relationships. My apartment is in the West Village, on Grove Street, a block south of Christopher Street, symbolic epicenter of the gay rights movement. In the 1970s, while my father was in Sweden and then subsequently back in California marrying my mother, gays in New York City were turning

Christopher Street into their Main Street. The gay bars and leather and whip shops that became a mainstay then are still here. I walk by them every day. I see gay couples holding hands and making out every weekend. After AIDS desecrated the gay community in the 1980s, gays moved north to Chelsea, but this is their history. This is where many found acceptance. I'm not gay, and I don't pretend to know what it would be like to be gay. But I did love someone who was gay, and it means everything to me in some small way to support him by living here. By surrounding myself with his community and his history. It's a neighborhood where my father would have been comfortable and where I feel at home. I feel close to him here. This is the home I built for myself in his memory. When Ben and I decide to live together, I am not yet ready to say goodbye to this home. Also, the bathroom is fabulous.

I'M ON A hill standing on a welcome mat somewhere outside Los Angeles in one of those small towns even most native Californians have never heard of, let alone been to. The welcome mat belongs to Sandy, a high school friend of my father's. I have driven six hours to meet her. I would have driven six hundred. I've been desperately trying to talk to anyone who knew him, but Sandy found me. She left a comment on my blog, and for the first time, I was thankful I had a blog. I press the doorbell and read the plaque above it. THE TIME TO BE HAPPY IS NOW, AND THE PLACE TO BE HAPPY IS HERE.

Sandy is tall with a wide face and highlighted brown hair that moves every time she opens her mouth. Everything about her is friendly: her eyes, her brightly colored blouse, and her voice, which is loud but in a reassuring way. I know I'll never miss a word. I try to be friendly. My father tried to be friendly. This woman standing in front of me doesn't have to try. Before I even say my name, she is enveloping me in a hug. Of course she hugs me. I should have known that was coming when I read her plaque.

I arrive thinking this interview is for me, but, now, I am not sure which one of us wants this more. She insists we open a bottle of wine. Even though it is only one o'clock, I am glad. Within five minutes, I know that she and her husband moved into this beautiful house on a hill only four months prior. Moreover, that they never would have been able to afford it if the house hadn't been in foreclosure. The wine we are drinking was on sale for four dollars at Costco. Or maybe it was Sam's Club. It isn't bad.

I adore her.

She has a trunk full of memories. We sit on the floor of a guest bedroom drinking our wine and sifting through the contents of that trunk for hours. She has yearbooks, reunion programs, ticket stubs, letters, photographs, and an endless stream of anecdotes. It is like she has always known I would show up someday. As if she has been waiting for me. I guess she has been.

Someone gave her my father's obituary, which mentioned only hospice care. She assumed he died of cancer. It wasn't until years later when she stumbled on something I had written for a newspaper about my father that she learned the true nature of his death. She asks me how his family responded to his illness and his homosexuality. I know the answer, but I don't respond immediately. I let the question hang between us. I'm not the only one with questions. We are interviewing each other.

"He told them he was HIV positive and gay at the same time. I don't know how they would have responded to the news he was gay if he wasn't also sick. The thought of losing him trumped whatever misgivings they might have had about homosexuality. His parents and his sisters were there for him until the end. His parents rose to the occasion."

She nods and says, "He was surrounded by love, then."

He was. We both were.

They stayed in touch for a while after high school. She moved to San Francisco, and my father visited her a few times. But her boyfriend didn't approve of her friends, and she and my father drifted apart. They saw each other at their ten-year high school reunion in 1980. My father brought my mom.

"He was so excited. He came with your mom, and he was just like he was in high school. Lots of energy and stories. He talked to everyone. It felt like no time had passed."

I imagine my father bouncing from conversation to conversation, his hands flying in animation. Smiling. When he felt like it, he could out-socialize an entire party. Only when I knew him, he didn't feel like it very often.

They saw each other again at their twenty-year high school reunion. This time my father came alone.

"He looked very sharp, very sophisticated that night. I'd never seen him dressed like that before. In high school, he was a bit wild. He had flair then." But it was more than just what he wore. "He spent most of the night talking to our friend Wayne. Some intense conversation they were having. No one interrupted them.

"We did talk, though. Briefly. I asked if he had any children. He showed me a picture of you. Little Victoria. That's what he called you. He said he was working in San Jose and that he went home to Sacramento on the weekends. I asked if you and your mom were going to move to San Jose. But he said no. He said it worked fine this way. He was so different than he had been at the last reunion in 'eighty."

"Different how?" I press her.

"Well. I said we should go out after for drinks. Catch up

some more. He didn't seem too interested. And later he just disappeared. He was gone. I wondered when Louis had become such a snob. That's the way I took it. He was distant. Unfriendly. I wondered why he didn't bring your mom."

"Could he have been shy? Maybe he felt uncomfortable?"

"What did he have to be shy about? Your dad didn't get uncomfortable," she answers quickly.

The man she knew probably didn't. The man she knew probably wasn't shy. But on the night of his twenty-year high school reunion, my father had been living with HIV for eleven months. He was no longer the man she knew. The new man, the one I remembered, could be shy, and he was often uncomfortable.

SHORTLY BEFORE MY father died, his sisters came. They took me out for breakfast. In the months before my father died, people were always taking me out. Everyone seemed to think this was a good idea. All I wanted was to stay with my dad.

They let me choose the restaurant. I took them to the diner my father and I used to go to every weekend. We sat in my father's favorite booth—the one close to the door so we could watch everyone come and go. His friends came in. Long hair. Long mustaches. Big muscles. Wraparound sunglasses. Leather vests. Denim. Hiking boots. The Hell's Angels. If the Angels were gay and liked orange marmalade on their pancakes. They walked right by our table. I didn't say hi. But I noticed where they sat and watched them like you watch a bee you don't want to sting you.

We went somewhere after breakfast. We picked something up or dropped something off. I don't remember. But when we got back to my father's house, his friends were there. They had come over after breakfast. My father asked if I had seen them at the restaurant. I nodded.

"Why didn't you say hi?"

"I was shy."

My father laughed. "You're not shy. There's never been anything shy about you."

His pronouncement startled me. I was shy a lot. He didn't know that?

I WANT TO find Wayne. The man Sandy said had had a long, intense conversation with my dad at their twenty-year high school reunion. I want to know what he and my father talked about. I wonder if my father confided in him. I hope so.

I track Wayne down through his mother, who is still living in Bakersfield. And the next thing I know Wayne and I are trading phone messages back and forth. When we finally connect, I am struck by the emotion in his voice. There is tenderness at the end of every syllable and I, perhaps naively, perhaps coldly, didn't anticipate that. Although they did not see or speak to each other in the second half of my father's life, it is immediately clear that they were once very close.

The words "best friend" had—up until this phone conversation—been just a convenient phrase. Wayne had been one of my father's groomsmen, and Sandy told me they had had that long intense conversation at their reunion, so I think of him as my father's best friend from high school. But what does that really mean? Maybe Wayne was just someone my father used to hang around with. My dad rarely allowed himself to get close to anyone, and it is hard to imagine that he might have let someone in as a teenager. I am convinced that in adolescence, with all its turbulence and heady drama, my father would surely have retreated. But then there was this supposed conversation in 1990.

Wayne and my father met, of all places, on the football field. They were thirteen-year-old boys who attended different middle schools but were both players in the Jack Frost Football League. My father was a defensive end. "Your dad was pretty good." But when they started freshman year at the same high school, my father didn't try out for the football team. "I didn't understand why. He would've made the team." While I'm surprised to learn my father not only knew how to play football but also was pretty good at the game, it doesn't surprise me that he didn't pursue it in high school.

Sandy told me that she remembers some of the jocks making fun of my dad.

"There were always rumors, you know. That he was gay. He had this way, like, he'd stand with his legs sort of intertwined. Like this."

We were sitting on the floor of a guest bedroom surrounded by old photos, letters, a graduation cap, and a baby sock belonging to a foot now grown. Sandy stood, a bit tipsy maybe, after all our discount wine, and demonstrated how my father used to stand. She crossed her right leg over her left so that her right calf was pressing into the shin of her left leg. I'd seen people stand this way but never my father. Maybe he had. I believed people had always suspected. I believe my father knew that. It was one thing to play for the Jack Frost Football League, but it would have been quite another to play for a large public high school's football team. My father might have been "pretty good" on the field, as Wayne claimed, but it was the bench and the locker room that I keep picturing. It is easier to imagine my father in a football uniform on the field than laughing and talking with the other guys on the bench or in the locker room after the game.

When my parents were married and I was a baby, they bought a house, and a couple who lived down the block invited them over for dinner with a few other couples. Years later, after my father had gotten sick and my parents separated, the wife told my mother that after my parents left that dinner party, everyone commented on the fact that my father was probably gay. It was a cruel thing to tell my mother, and I can't imagine what that woman thought she was accomplishing, but it wasn't the first time my father had left such an impression in his wake. A few relatives and family friends claim they knew. I don't know what's worse: that these people suspected and gossiped about it and never told my mother, or that my father was desperately trying to keep secret a fact that was obvious to so many.

Wayne is kind. He tells me that my father brought him out of his jock existence. They saw *A Clockwork Orange* and *2001: A Space Odyssey* together. My father convinced him to sneak onto campus over spring break and disconnect all the school bells. They ran the high school literary magazine together. They double-dated.

"Your dad was very sexually active in high school. He was always dating women. They were attracted to him even though . . . effeminate is too strong of a word. But he had a kind of mild, gentle side to him, you know?"

Gentle? That is not a word I would have used to describe my father, but I wish it were. I'm glad that Wayne thought of my father that way.

Before I can ask Wayne what he and my dad talked about at their high school reunion, he tells me that he kept going to their high school reunions because he was always hoping he would run into my dad. But he never did. I tell him that my father was at the reunion in 1990, and I ask if he attended that year. He says that he did but that he doesn't remember seeing my dad.

Memory is a tricky thing.

I wonder what my father remembered of the reunion. If he remembers Sandy or Wayne. If he really left abruptly like Sandy said. I wonder why he went. Or if he was ever really there at all.

Wayne tells me my father enjoyed being a part of the world. His choice of words is not lost on me, and I am both so sorry that my father lost that joy and so glad that he had it once.

"You know, I attribute a lot of my appreciation for art to your dad. He taught me a lot, and he took me places I wouldn't have otherwise gone. I visited him in college, and we went to the Pasadena Museum [of California Art], and your dad said something to me that, at the time, I just didn't get at all. He said, 'The negative space helps define the positive space.' I stood there looking at him as if he was from another planet."

I think about my father as a nineteen-year-old college kid standing in a Southern California modern art museum espousing on negative and positive space, repeating what he read in a textbook or heard in class. He could have been speaking about his own life and future: ultimately, the negative space (or negative people, circumstances, choices, accidents, feelings) in his life did define the positive space (or positive people, circumstances, choices, accidents, feelings). It destroyed it.

Wayne told me that he and my father were the editors of their high school literary magazine, *HUZZA!* The magazines they produced and created arrive in the mail two days after we speak. My father's drawings are in all three publications, but it is the issue from their senior year, when my father was the editor, that I can't stop looking at. The magazine is modeled after the 1920s with a series of photographs of the six-person editorial staff dressed in 1920s-appropriate attire. According to Wayne, the idea was my father's. He convinced the rest of the staff to dress up, and they took pictures at the old train station in downtown Bakersfield.

On the cover of *HUZZA!*, my father and his fellow literati members stare stone-faced at the camera in their costumes. Wayne is standing in the middle, solemn in his bow tie and gunless shoulder holsters. My father stands beside Wayne on the end. His posture is ramrod straight and his shoulders are back, his feet spread wide apart. He is wearing a dark suit and leather driving gloves. A cigar dangles from his mouth. His head is cocked back to the side and his eyes are slits; he looks out at the camera as if to say, *What the hell do you want?* It is clearly a seventeen-year-old boy's idea of a gangster.

On the inside cover is a photo my father took of Wayne. He is standing at the sink in a public bathroom. Across the tile wall he is writing "HUZZA!" On the following page is the preface, written by my father as the magazine's editor. In it, he explains the magazine's theme:

> A new idea we did decide on was giving the magazine a new look—the old look of the 1920s. This era represents the free, unique attitudes of the staff of the *HUZZA!* These were the attitudes that kept us going, and the attitudes that got us in the most trouble!

Other photos appear throughout the magazine between poems and short stories: the staff pretending to fistfight atop an old train, posing on the steps of an old saloon, peering out between the bars in the window of the old jail. In every one, my father has his cigar and that same slit-eye stare. In another photo, my father and Wayne pose side by side outside the old jail. They are shoulder to shoulder, and Wayne is leaning into my dad, and they are both scowling. And in one of the final shots in the book, my father and Wayne and another boy are being held up by a fourth. A girl lies in front of them, "shot down." My father and Wayne and the other boy have their arms up in surrender. My father's still got his cigar hanging out of his mouth. But this time, he's trying, and failing, to hide a smile. He loves this make-believe and the ingenuity of the photo shoot—his idea, after all. It is plain—the cracking smile and the glint in his eye—that he is having fun.

And on the back cover, a white page and a single quote: "TO WHOM IT MAY CONCERN: FATE."

In this magazine and these photos, I see proof of what my father's friends have been trying to tell me; he was happy once.

I show the book to Ben, pointing out the pictures of my father. He squints. "You look like him," he says. I look like my happy father. I can't help but smile.

18

◆ ⋅⋮⋅ ◆

WINTERS IN THE SACRAMENTO VALLEY ARE wet and dark. The trees are barren, the sky inhospitable gray. The roads are slick with the residue of a dense and dirty, slippery rainfall—you spend the months until spring trying to hold on. It was the winter before my father's death, and I was ten years old. I was walking home from school, and I decided to surprise him at his house. I slipped through the side gate into the backyard for the spare key. But it wasn't there. I knocked on the glass bedroom door that led out to the yard. My father waved, motioning for me to get the key. I shouted through the glass that it was missing. "Look again. It's there," he replied. I looked under the potted plants, still heavy with recent rain, and under the bronzed steel patio furniture that my father no longer used. I returned to the glass door empty-handed. I watched him struggle to stand and come to me, to reach a doorknob less than two feet from his bed. He fell back against the pillows, and pill bottles bounced in the sheets. Two fell to the floor. He did not try to retrieve them. I could see his chest falling and thrusting out, as he attempted to catch his breath. *Try again. Please.* He heaved himself upward and onto his feet, only to begin shaking. His knees buckled. He was on the floor. His back was to me. He did not turn, but after a moment, he raised his trembling hand and dismissed me. I walked home to my mother's. When I got there, I didn't call him. I didn't get someone to help him, either—that would have enraged him. He wouldn't have wanted anyone else to know. I understood it was to be another secret.

My father hated help. No one else could ever do a job as well as he could. A week before, my father had wanted eggs Benedict. When he had still been able to go out for breakfast, it was the dish he almost always ordered. Now, he had to rely on the part-time nurse, who had never even heard of eggs Benedict. She scurried back and forth between his bedroom and the kitchen, as my father dictated the recipe. But he wasn't clear enough. He didn't tell her to slice the English muffin in two before assembling the eggs and meat and hollandaise sauce. When she nervously laid the tray on his lap, my father was furious.

He couldn't cook anymore, and now, he couldn't even stand up and open a door. He was humiliated. I knew we would never discuss the incident. I felt sorry for my father, who was watching his life slip out of his grasp, piece by piece. Every day he lost something new, and it seemed to me that it would go on that way, lose a memory here, lose a skill there, like saying goodbye to a finger, to a big toe and an earlobe, until nothing remained but a dip in the mattress where he had lain for so many months.

We spent my father's last Christmas in his hometown. The Bakersfield my family and I knew was the kind of oppressive valley community in which everyone had a swimming pool and drove a white car. You'd be a fool to drive a black car in that heat. I recall little of the days leading up to the holiday, but my grandparents did take me to Dewar's, a local candy shop and soda fountain. I loved Dewar's. My father had gone there as a child with his sisters and, later, his friends. He even worked for a time in high school as a bag boy at the grocery store across the street. Dewar's was crowded. We sat at the counter on stools that twirled. I always ordered a tan and white sundae, which was an excessive concoction of vanilla ice cream, caramel sauce, and chocolate ice cream all topped decadently with whipped marshmallows. It was my father's favorite. He'd attempt to swipe spoonfuls from my sundae, and I would protest loudly until I could eat no more. I'd sheepishly push it his way, and he'd finish it for me. That year, my father was too sick to come. My mother came, though, like she always did. We sat side by side. But the tan and white wasn't her favorite, and she was content to eat only her single scoop of mint chocolate chip. I ate very little. My sundae melted into a sticky, taupe soup, and, eventually, the man behind the counter took it away.

"Are you okay?" my mom asked.

"Yeah."

"Not hungry?"

"Not really," I said.

She tucked a piece of my hair behind my ear, which normally would have annoyed me. But her soft fingertips grazed my temple, and it felt nice. She put her arm around my shoulders, leaned down, and said, "That's just fine." Her breath smelled of mint, cool and sweet.

WE CELEBRATED THE holiday at my father's younger sister's house. Her husband made margaritas, which is what you drink on Christmas in California in our family. From the kitchen came the smell of fresh-squeezed limes and the sound of the blender barking and hissing. From the family room, the music of my cousins' video game reverberated. I don't remember where my aunts and my mom were, but they were usually together. My father always said my mother fit in better with his family than he did.

In the living room, my father and I were silent.

People walked around us carrying drinks or holding a child's hand, but none of them were real to me. I sat on the couch looking out through the sliding glass doors at the pool and the dogs lying in the sun. My father had been tucked into the easy chair next to the couch. His skin was thin and taut like Saran Wrap preserving leftovers. A ratty brown-and-orange blanket his grandmother had knit decades ago hung from his knees. On his head, over the scabs and sores on his pale scalp, someone had knotted a silk scarf. He looked like a gypsy off her rocker.

We said nothing. My father began to sob. I had never seen him cry, and I did not want to now. His face was red, almost purple, and he shook, heaving violently and loudly. He pressed his fists into his thighs, and I knew they would leave bruises behind. He didn't have the strength for tears. He couldn't breathe and cry. *He's going to die of sorrow.*

One of my cousins nudged the family room door shut, muffling the video game gunshots and the sound of the cartoon figures punching each other with the blunt end of machine guns. I heard the music change abruptly, and I knew one of the characters had died.

My grandfather appeared in the doorway. He was tall and dark after a lifetime spent in the sun, and he looked every bit the retired Republican sheriff of Kern County he was. He had the steadiness of a man who was accustomed to being in charge, a man who knew how to control a situation without shouts or punches. His presence soothed me, though he remained motionless in the doorway, neither in the room nor out of it. He watched his middle child, his only son.

My father stumbled through a few slurred regrets about never being able to see his nephews grow up and about all the disappointment and trouble he had caused. The words stopped.

His head fell, and his tears dropped, one by one, into his lap. My grandfather stepped forward. He adjusted the blanket around my father's protruding shoulder blades, knelt, and pulled his son close so that their foreheads kissed.

When my father had no more tears to shed, my grandfather stood up. He looked at me, and I looked at him. As he walked by me, he placed his fingertips on the top of my head. I listened to his footsteps retreat down the hall and had to hold myself back from running after him. *Papa, don't go.*

My father sank back into the cushioned chair. He seemed ancient. He was forty-three. He didn't look at me. I wished I had cried with him. I wanted to say something. I wanted to slide across the couch and down onto the carpet so that I could sit on the floor and feel his leg against my arm. I wanted to feel the heat from his body against my own. I wanted him to be glad I was beside him. But I did not move. I was afraid he didn't want me to touch him. Worse, I was afraid he wouldn't acknowledge my touch. We sat, wordless. He looked at the wall, and I gazed at him, until I worried that he would turn and catch me and tell me to go play with my cousins. I closed my eyes, feigning sleep; I was afraid, but I wanted to stay.

A few months before, a friend's father had told me that all his life he knew he wanted to have three children, and in fact, he was a proud father of three daughters. For weeks afterward, I wondered if my parents had always only wanted one. Finally, over breakfast in a café, long after I had finished my oatmeal and grown bored watching my father linger over the newspaper and yet another coffee refill, I asked.

"Daddy . . . how many kids did you want?"

"What a strange question, kiddo."

"Did you always want one?"

"I didn't want any."

"Oh."

"I didn't think I wanted kids until I held you in the hospital. Then I knew."

"Why?"

"Why what?"

"Why did you want me after you held me?"

"You were perfect. Your eyes were the same size, your nose wasn't too big or too small, and your lips were full and pink. Nothing was out of place; you were beautiful. I couldn't get over you, that's how I knew."

"Oh . . . I'm glad I wasn't really ugly."

He hadn't wanted to be a father at all. But once he knew my mother was pregnant, he hoped they would have a son. He told me this not long after our conversation in the café. He told me, because I asked. He was in bed, and I sat on my backpack on the floor. We were studying our family trees in school, and I had learned that my last name stopped with me. I asked my father if this bothered him.

"Sure, I was upset. I wanted a boy."

I left him, went to my room, and threw a tennis ball against the back of the door. Each time the yellow ball sprang back and slammed into my palm, I lobbed it again at the door. Again and again, it thudded against the wood, and I relished the thud until my mother angrily crashed into the room.

"What are you doing? This isn't a tennis court. You're upsetting your father."

"Exactly."

My father saw little value in softening the truth for the sake of my feelings. He lied about his sexuality not to protect the people who loved him but to protect himself. What *he* wanted, what *he* needed was paramount. He hurt me, and I wanted to hurt him back.

But he was hurting plenty without my help. By that last Christmas, he had lost his dark curls, which would never turn white. His body, formerly strong and lean from his many hours at the gym, had withered, leaving behind open sores, chapped skin, and a bluish, hollow shell. He was practically bedridden, and he took handfuls of pills throughout the day.

We remained in my aunt's house sitting not beside each other, but near one another—both together and apart—until it was time to leave. Someone stacked the presents in the trunk of the car, and someone else placed Tupperware containers of holiday remains in the backseat, cold roast and pie. My mother was in the car with the engine running and the heat on high, because my father was never warm anymore. My grandfather held my father's hand to steady him. Together they walked outside to the car, and my grandfather helped his son into the passenger seat. My aunts came for me. They rested their palms against my cheeks, and I opened my eyes. "Are you tired?" they asked. "No," I replied. "We are," they said.

I sat in the backseat behind my father. We drove by a 7-Eleven. I wanted a Coke Slurpee, but I knew enough not to ask. It was late and dark, and my mother drove below the speed limit. The streets were empty and bare; it didn't feel like Christmas.

19

You'd have to be a real asshole not to like Paris. I am that asshole. Video chatting with Ben, I mention something about a restaurant in the West Village that I know he doesn't like because he's not big on Middle Eastern food. I don't know how it came up, but it did. He immediately claims he never said that. That he loves Middle Eastern food. Despite the fact every time I suggest this restaurant, he counters with another idea. Another cuisine. Despite the fact I have a distinct memory of the conversation and of his words. I insist he did say it, but he just says, "You're crazy." I get upset. Don't call me crazy! Sometimes, when my mom and I fight, she will tell me, "Get a grip." Ben telling me I'm crazy feels exactly like my mom telling me to get a grip. Nothing feels more dismissive. Nothing makes me feel more like I know nothing. As if I can count on nothing. He doesn't understand why I'm so upset.

"If recent conversations I swear took place are actually figments of my imagination, what does that say about *everything* I think I remember about my father?!"

I want very much for Ben to be wrong, but he's adamant, and I'm doubting myself. We have a terse video goodbye. I try to write, but my fingers hover paralyzed over the keyboard.

So I walk. I walk from the Jardin du Luxembourg to Les Puces de Paris Saint-Ouen, the famous Paris flea market, where I wander through a maze of stalls full of everything that makes up a rich life: silver, baby christening gowns, armoires, metal yo-yos, silk thread, porcelain urns. When my eyes glaze over, I turn around and walk to the Louvre. I never feel lost, never confused. Somehow, I know this city. It reminds me a bit of New York, as many others before me have observed. But it's something else. I recognized this city almost instantly, and I know I didn't feel that way when I met New York for the first time.

I keep walking.

From the Louvre, I walk to the Shakespeare and Company bookstore in the Left Bank, to the Pantheon, and, finally, to the 4th arrondissement to eat at L'As du Fallafel, because everyone, but especially Mark Bittman of *The New York Times*, claims it will be the best falafel of my life. I for one like Middle Eastern food. Only L'As du Fallafel is closed. It is closed without explanation. It's not a Saturday, on which, in observance of the Sabbath, they are always closed. I did my research. I know its hours. L'As du Fallafel is supposed to be open. But it's not.

I am starving and tired and now here come the tears. Ugly, fat, American tears. I am frustrated because I'm supposed to be eating the best falafel of my entire life, and I'm not. I've already been starving for an hour, ignoring every patisserie and fromagerie on my walk. There were a lot of them. Idiotic? Absolutely. But an irrational part of my brain needs every meal to be the best meal of my life. Every meal counts so much. The thought of eating a mediocre ham and cheese croissant from a random patisserie that no one on Chowhound has ever raved about in all capital letters and with excessive exclamation points would feel like an epic failure.

Sure, you could persuasively argue that letting myself get

so hungry I end up sobbing in the middle of the street is its own epic failure. Ben would make that argument. Ben. I'm upset that I fought with my sweet boyfriend over video chat. I wish, at the very least, we'd fought in person.

He had wanted to meet me in Paris, but I told him it was a bad idea. I thought I should be focused on my dad and the trip he and I would have taken together. Being here was about my dad, not Ben. Wasn't it? But now I was here alone realizing what everybody else seems to know intuitively: Paris is not a city to meet alone. Sure, you can come to Paris by yourself. But not for the first time. And the thing is, I'm not a little girl anymore. Whatever trip my father and I would have taken here, it's gone. This, me, standing outside a tiny falafel shop crying to and for myself, no more resembles that haunting vacation than being here with Ben would have. Being with Ben would be so much more fun.

I know I hurt his feelings. He wanted to come. But I told him no. It might have been the right decision, but it doesn't feel right.

He is not the first boyfriend who has wanted to go to Paris with me. There was another boyfriend, also named Ben. We met in Michigan one summer when we were working for the same hotel on Mackinac Island. He was tall and broad and had Superman's strong jaw. He was a few years out of college, and I had graduated mere days before I flew to Michigan. We were untethered. Our jobs would end in October, and what? Ben had majored in French in college. He wanted us to go to Paris.

In bed, he whispered sweet nothings in French to me. He told me again and again how much I would love it. But the more he told me, the more I pulled away. Until we stopped having sex. Until I was practically avoiding him. I was terrified at the thought of seeing Paris for the first time with a man I hardly knew who had swept me off my feet in the haze and uncertainty of a summer romance. Irresponsible. I only had one opportunity to see Paris for the first time. I couldn't screw it up. At the end of the summer, I went back to New York. We didn't break up, exactly. We didn't say goodbye. We just returned to our real lives.

We kept in touch, and I was happy to know this Ben. Superman, as I called him. But I was relieved that we had not gone to Paris together. Paris was still safe.

IN CAMBODIA, I was mourning and only just beginning to heal. William and I had finally said goodbye, and for the first time in my adult life I was facing my father and my memories of him head on. There, my mission was clear: to be my father's eyes and ears, to show his memory—his legacy at least—Angkor Wat.

In Stockholm, I had letters and photos and an address, and it was comforting to think I was walking where he once walked. I was seeing and hearing sights and sounds he had once heard. With every step I walked in that city, I felt my father's shadow. I felt him reaching across the thirty-nine years that separated his time in Stockholm and my own. I saw the city both as it is in the present day and as it might have been in 1972.

But in Paris, I'm not fulfilling a lifelong dream of my father's. I have no letters, no address, and no photographs to guide me through his visit here with Daniel. Paris is for me. It was going to be my father's gift to me. But how do you accept a gift from someone who isn't here to give it to you?

I feel lost in this old city. Haunted. It is a beautiful place, but I can't help thinking how incredible it would have been to see it with my father. To have him show me Paris. He would have loved eating the morning's soft-boiled egg from a porcelain eggcup. He would have approved of the French talent for lingering over meals and the way Parisians make lingering feel like a respectable activity. He would have applauded Velib', the public bicycle share system, and we would have used it constantly. I resent having to show myself. Every bridge, every baguette, every park is a reminder of what he didn't show me, of what we didn't do together. I still don't know what it would have felt like to take a walk in Paris with my dad.

Had I let Ben come with me, it might have been easier to ignore this loss. But I didn't, and now I am surrounded by the past—both my own and this city's—and I find these two pasts converging on me, moving in closer and closer. In Stockholm, seeing buildings and places that I know my father once saw was comforting. It made me feel closer to him. He was just a kid in Stockholm, and it was his first time abroad. He built a life for himself there, and I got a glimpse of it. But when he went to Paris he had been with Daniel and in love. It was a whirlwind trip that only the two of them shared.

In Paris I feel farther away from him than ever.

In Siem Reap and Stockholm, I could sit for hours, content to watch and smell and taste the unfamiliar world around me. But I spend my time in Paris moving. I walk from one end of the city to the other and back. I can't seem to stop moving. And that is what I know of Paris: the walking. Don't stop.

I ACCEPT THAT L'As du Fallafel is closed and begin the long walk back to the apartment I have rented. Though I have been walking all day, it is only now, through teary, blurry vision, that I realize why this city feels so familiar. It reminds me of my father. Paris is tall, dark, and handsome, but it also feels a bit like walking through a museum. Everything is behind glass, and you're not allowed to touch anything. Even in the summer it's just a little uncomfortable. A little too cold—like a restaurant. I know this is unfair—I hardly know this town—and I'm undoubtedly wrong, but it seems to me that, unlike New York City, there is only one Paris: everything and everyone is the same.

There are people who wear their lives on their faces. When you meet them you learn their names and their histories all in a breath and a glance. You can see their years of sunbathing, their acne scars, their suspicions and joys. You can tell they're about to smile a second before they do, and you know immediately when they're offended or confused. New York is one of these people.

There are other people who have but a single face and expression for the world. Their eyes stare right through you, and you never know what they're thinking or what they're going to do or what they've thought in the past or done in all the moments leading up to meeting you. They are distant, and you may know them for years without ever feeling like you know them at all. Paris is one of these people. My father was one of these people. Paris is holding me at arm's length.

20

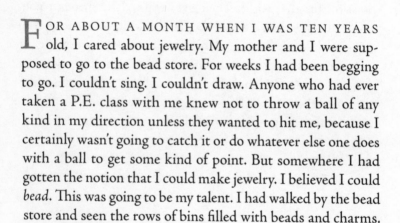

For about a month when I was ten years old, I cared about jewelry. My mother and I were supposed to go to the bead store. For weeks I had been begging to go. I couldn't sing. I couldn't draw. Anyone who had ever taken a P.E. class with me knew not to throw a ball of any kind in my direction unless they wanted to hit me, because I certainly wasn't going to catch it or do whatever else one does with a ball to get some kind of point. But somewhere I had gotten the notion that I could make jewelry. I believed I could *bead*. This was going to be my talent. I had walked by the bead store and seen the rows of bins filled with beads and charms, each brightly colored and shiny like the syrupy, hard candies on my great-grandmother's coffee table. Finally, the Saturday before my eleventh birthday, we were going.

I had left the front door open and was standing on the porch. Waiting. My mother was rushing through the living room toward me, and I was giving her attitude with my eyes. The phone rang. "Don't answer it," I said. It had rung before, while I was putting on my shoes. I hadn't understood the woman on the other end. She had been hysterical. I had hung up. Ignored it. But now it was ringing again. My mother answered. I couldn't hear the conversation. I leaned against the porch railing looking out onto the street. I heard her behind me. She hurried by me to the driveway. "Get in the car. Your father. Donna found him."

We drove the four blocks to my father's house. I asked questions.

"Is he dead?"

"Not yet."

"Okay."

"Donna said his pill bottles were empty. His gun was on the bed."

"Daddy has a gun?"

"A handgun. Your grandfather gave it to me when Daddy moved out. I didn't want it in the house. So I gave it to Daddy."

"Did he use it?"

"No. He just held it."

I pictured my father swallowing fistfuls of pills. I pictured him curling up beneath his satin sheets cradling a gun in his bony, brittle arms.

We pulled up behind the ambulance. Its doors were flung open, and men in navy polos were pushing a gurney inside. I couldn't see anything beyond these men. Donna, my father's nurse, was in the front yard. Just then, I hated her. Her job was over; she'd pack up her bag and go home and soon enough we would be foggy in her mind, just another dead client and his family.

Two of the EMTs jumped into the ambulance behind the gurney. I saw my father's shape then, a body beneath a white sheet. I wanted to see his nose and mouth; I wanted to know that his face was under the sheet, but I couldn't see that far into the ambulance. Only the bottoms of his bare feet were visible. I knew those feet. They were my feet, too. He had given them to me. We shared overstuffed feet that spread out wide and pudgy when we got out of bed in the morning. His looked frail now, and cold. Why hadn't anyone pulled the sheet down and tucked it under his heels? I stared at his exposed skin. I was embarrassed for my father. He was private, careful about what others knew and saw. There was a time when he had given the impression of dignity—his long neck rose out of his crisp, collared shirts and his slender fingers sliced the air with grace when he wanted to make his point emphatic. I thought of his eyes, the color of dark cherries, and how they had rarely looked directly at me, but beyond me, at something innocuous, like a lamp or the arm of a chair. Now, here, on this dreary March day, as his neighbors peeked through their lace curtains, he was outside, vulnerable, lying beneath only a flimsy sheet. All these women saw his feet. They saw his toes, sticking straight up in the air, and his soles, which after months of bed rest were tender and pink. Who were these aged women sucking on nicotine and blowing it out against their windowpanes? They had no right to see his feet. I wanted out of my seat belt and out of the car. I wanted to climb into the ambulance, shut the doors, and hold his feet in my lap against the warmth of my palms. An EMT slammed the door, and the ambulance wheels began to turn. My mother started the car, and we followed his feet.

At the hospital, we waited. My father was taken away, and my mother was interrogated in a tiny room; I learned later they suspected my father had not acted alone and that my mother had assisted him. I sat by myself in the hallway in a green vinyl chair. Nurses hustled back and forth between their desks and the long row of beds, each curtained off to give the illusion of privacy. My father was behind one of those curtains, but I did not know which one. I felt like a game show contestant. If I pushed aside the right curtain, I would find my father sitting up on the gurney wearing silk pajamas and cheering along with the studio audience. He'd be holding my prize-winning blender. I stared at each curtain. There were fifteen. An old woman stepped out from behind one. One down, fourteen to go.

I played this game until thoughts of a conversation my father and I had had only a few weeks earlier came rushing back. He said, "Remember when we watched that one movie with Ted Danson and Whoopi Goldberg and you said Whoopi Goldberg was beautiful and I said that wasn't true? Well, you were right and I was wrong and I'm sorry."

It was a Sunday morning in late February, and I was curled up on his bed using a marker to draw unibrows and soul patches on the photographs of people in the Sunday paper. My father was working on the sports section; he often gave the athletes devil horns and curly mustaches. For years, on weekend mornings, we lingered at the dining room table over maple bacon and frittatas, rendering the subjects of the newspaper pictures unrecognizable. But in the months since my father had been bedridden and stopped eating much of anything besides pills and Ensure, I brought the paper and a box of cereal to his bed every Sunday morning instead. Now he was apologizing to me. This was a first.

I turned the page and ate a raisin from the Just Right cereal box.

"*Made in America*. The name of the movie with Ted Danson and Whoopi Goldberg was *Made in America*," I said.

I gave Vice President Al Gore a nose ring before continuing. "What made you change your mind?"

"My interpretation of beauty was too narrow, I think. I still say most people probably don't consider her beautiful, but we do," he replied.

My father was not a rash man. Every decision he made, whether it was which brand of milk to buy or where to live, was based on research and logic and involved long, detailed explanations that made you regret asking in the first place. He wouldn't commit to suicide on a whim. It wasn't just a bad day. What he feared most was powerlessness, and he knew that if he didn't kill himself, he would eventually no longer be able to open a pill bottle or pull a trigger on his own. He would be wholly at the mercy of his disease.

By that Sunday morning the caregivers had already been coming for weeks. They cooked in his kitchen, read magazines in his study, and smoked on his porch. If he was thirsty, they got him water. If he needed to use the bathroom, they held his hand and propped his body up against their own. He was running out of time. He was apologizing about Whoopi because he knew it was time to start saying whatever needed to be said. I like to think that he just didn't know how to apologize for getting sick or never saying he loved me; so, instead, he did the next best thing—he told me I was right. He told me Whoopi Goldberg was a babe. But maybe I'm wrong. Maybe he really thought the only thing he had to apologize for was a difference of opinion we'd had over an actress's physical appearance two years prior. I didn't know, and I knew I'd never really know. I leaned my head against his shoulder, and said, "Yeah, I was right."

A hospital nurse startled me out of my thoughts. I could join my mother in the tiny room now. As soon as I entered, I knew it was the bad-news room. Someone had made a pathetic attempt to humanize it, to mask the percolating hospital smell of decay with cheap potpourri. A love seat and chair had been shoved into opposite corners, and a Monet poster had been taped to the wall. My mother sat on the love seat and a doctor sat in the chair. I sat down next to my mother. She told me my father had not wanted to be resuscitated. "Now what?" I asked. She and the doctor exchanged a look. "We wait," she said. *For him to die,* I thought. The doctor asked if I wanted to see him. I said I did. "That's not a good idea," my mother said. We looked at each other. "I don't want his feet to be the last part of him I see, Mom."

* * *

HE WAS BEHIND curtain number seven. A nurse yanked the curtain closed behind me, and we were alone. They had moved him onto a bed. I stood at the foot of it, not yet ready to go forward. His feet were still bare. I wrapped my hands around them. They were icy. "Daddy, your feet are so cold." I rubbed hard against his skin, trying to bring him warmth. I studied the few dark, wiry hairs on his big toes. They were long and coarse, and they alone seemed alive. I tucked his feet under the blanket, but I remained at the foot of the bed and thought of the "when game" we used to play.

It took him many years to let me pour my own milk for my cereal in the mornings. He didn't like a mess, and he didn't trust my hand-eye coordination. Instead, he poured for me. "Tell me when, Victoria." I'd watch the milk soak the granola medley and slowly fill the bowl. "When, Daddy." And he'd stop. In the months after he was bedridden, late in the evenings after the caregiver had gone home for the day, my father would sometimes ask for a snack. He liked strawberries in milk sprinkled with a little bit of sugar. In the kitchen, I'd cut the stems off the berries and use a teaspoon to add the sugar. But I'd wait to pour the milk until I got to his bedroom and he cupped the bowl in his hands. "Tell me when, Daddy." I'd begin to pour, but soon, because he never liked a lot, he would say, "When, Victoria." And I'd stop.

I moved from the foot of the bed to the head. I laid my hand on top of his. His skin was dry. His eyes were open but solid, blocked like a wall. "It's my birthday on Thursday." I squeezed his fingers to feel his skin tight against mine. "I'm going to be eleven." I looked around. Maybe it was silly to talk to him. I knew he couldn't hear me. But what if he could? Just because he couldn't talk didn't mean he couldn't listen. Right? I lowered my voice. "I'm having this murder mystery–themed party. Did I tell you? Everyone's a suspect. We all have different characters and like different bios and stuff and everyone has to dress up. There's a script, too, but no one can read it before the party. We have to act everything out and figure out what happened, why the victim died." I let go of his hand. I swallowed. "It's a game."

I didn't want to be there anymore. But I forced myself to lean down and kiss him at the corner of his mouth. He smelled putrid but I didn't pull away. I rested my cheek against his and whispered into his ear, "When, Daddy. It's okay. When."

I stepped outside and pulled the curtain closed. I didn't want to be there anymore, but I didn't want to leave him, either. I didn't want to say goodbye. The nurse who had brought me was nowhere to be seen. Patients and families and doctors and nurses rushed by. I stood guard at his curtain. I stood there until my mother appeared, trailing behind yet another nurse. This nurse wheeled my father to a private room on a higher floor. My mother and I followed obediently. The room had real walls and a window that looked out onto a state park where I had spent the night on a class trip the year before. The nurse left, and it was just the three of us. This was our family. It was the last time we would be together. My mother sat down in a chair next to the bed. I paced. I looked out the window and down at the street and the park below. Cars drove by. Children ran across the grass. It was not until I caught my tear-stained reflection in the window that I realized I was crying. I let the tears fall. Now we sat and waited for my father to stop breathing. When that happened, my mother would notify the nurses' station, a doctor would come, and my father's death would be pronounced and recorded. We didn't know how long this would take. Probably only hours. But how many?

My mother called the parents of a friend of mine. They parked on the street below my father's window, and I watched them file out of their minivan. The entire family came—mother, father, sons, daughter—like a brigade. They took me back to their home. I didn't want them to, but I had misplaced my voice. We sat on the couch in their family room watching *Beverly Hills, 90210* reruns. Someone made popcorn, and the family dog stood at my feet hoping to catch an errant kernel or two. Later, someone turned on *The Princess Bride*. I had spent hundreds of Saturday nights in my friend's house doing just those things over the years, and that night was no different. The popcorn tasted good. *The Princess Bride* made me laugh. But I was angry, too. Angry that my mother had dismissed me and that I wasn't allowed to stay with her and my father. So I had fun and I got mad and I embraced every emotion except sorrow.

A day passed by the time my mother came.

IT WAS MORNING when she picked me up. I heard the doorbell. My friend and I were upstairs sprawled across her four-poster bed reading *Cosmopolitan*. I heard my mother's voice, but I didn't get up. My friend was quoting from an article—something about blowjobs—and we were giggling. I was both giggling and listening to my mother's steps on the staircase. She was coming. She opened the door. My friend's mom was behind her, and very quickly my friend slid off the bed and left with her mom, as though some secret signal had been given. I remained on my stomach stretched out across the comforter. My mother leaned against the bed beside me.

"Where is he?" I asked.

"The hospital or the funeral home. If not now, soon."

"Are you sure he's dead?"

My mother nodded.

"Did you tell Grandma and Papa?"

My mother nodded again.

"When is the funeral?"

"Thursday," she replied.

"I want to go home."

We walked the block and a half home. We moved with care under tree branches hanging low and dogs doing their business. It wasn't hot, and it wasn't cold. There was the crack in the sidewalk where I fell long ago and my father picked me up, bloody-kneed and teary-eyed. I stepped over the crack and remembered being in his arms with my snotty nose pressed against his chest, enveloped in his scent, equal parts leather and brown butter. We crossed the street, and I saw him wearing his aviators in his convertible on a warm day with the radio blasting the rapper Nas. My mother and I walked in silence. There was nothing to say.

For seven years my father battled AIDS, and for seven years we knew he would eventually lose. For seven years we held our breath and watched him deteriorate. This morning we could breathe again. He wasn't suffering anymore and no longer would our lives revolve around illness and the specter of death. I followed my mother up our driveway and onto the porch. We stood together with our backs to the house, not yet ready to go inside, looking out at our street. It was Sunday morning. We stared straight ahead, avoiding each other's gaze, but reassured by the other's presence. "He's finally free," my mother said.

21

———— ✦ ⋮ ✦ ————

WE HAD MY FATHER'S FUNERAL SERVICE AT
the Catholic church my mother and I attended, the
church connected to my elementary school. My mother requested a full Mass. My father was not Catholic, and the Mass
would have meant little to him, but my first lesson in funerals
was that they are for the living. The Mass meant something to
my mom. I was an altar server at our church, and our priest
asked if I'd like to serve at my father's Mass. I knew how to
be an altar girl. What I didn't know was how to attend my
father's funeral. I said yes—I would treat it like just another
Mass, going through the rituals, waiting for my cues to light
the candles, ring the bells, wash the priest's hands.

At the start of the service, I entered ahead of the priest,
carrying the cross. I carried Jesus on that heavy wooden cross
in front of me like a shield. I led the priest down the aisle and
up the steps to the altar. I looked at no one. I knew almost
every face. For the few I didn't, they knew mine. My father's
friend Marion is the only person I remember from the church.
She was to give one of the eulogies, and she sat on the altar in
a chair beside the pulpit. I remember her dress. She held her
hands in her lap waiting to speak. She gave an eloquent eulogy, but it was hard to listen, because I knew I was next. I was

going to read a poem. When she was done, she sat back down in the chair near the pulpit, and I walked up to take her place.

At the funeral home, we had been given a thick binder of appropriate memorial readings. I announced that I wanted to read something at the service, and my mother slid the book across the table to me. I flipped through it as if it were a magazine while she made whatever arrangements needed to be made for my father's cremation. It was a photo album, only instead of pictures there were hundreds of sad poems, quotes, and song lyrics tucked into glossy plastic sleeves. I chose quickly. There was a correct answer, and I would get it right. I knew I'd found it as soon as I read the first line: "Don't grieve for me, for now I'm free." Then, near the end: "Perhaps my time seemed all too brief, / Don't lengthen it now with undue grief." An admonishment. It sounded good. My father was free, and we were so happy for him, we weren't going to feel too much pain! I wanted to follow directions. I just never could have guessed how miserably I'd come to fail at this particular task. Years later I realized the poem is a ubiquitous funeral reading. Not that anyone could have ever convinced me of that in the days leading up to my father's Mass. It was his poem, and I read it over and over again until I knew it better than I knew the Lord's Prayer and the Pledge of Allegiance and all the other declarations I was raised to make.

IN THE SEVENTEEN months after my father's death and cremation, my mother spent more hours at work than at home, and I chopped off my hair because I wanted to look as bad as I felt. My father sat, meanwhile, in a cardboard box on a closet shelf. The day my mother and I retrieved him from the funeral home, the director reminded us to keep the box up high, away from any pets, particularly cats. We were too dazed to ask why; we simply nodded. On the way to the car, my mother carried my father gingerly, as if he wasn't already broken, before placing him on the passenger seat and fastening his seat belt. At home, she put him on his appointed shelf in the closet, where he began to collect dust. We did not talk of him except to joke that after so many years as a closeted gay man, my father had died, only to be shoved back into the closet. We laughed, but not because we found it funny.

Sometimes I would visit him in the closet. It comforted me to see that cardboard box and say to myself, "There. He's there." I came to feel that we had imprisoned him on that shelf, and finally my mother and I began to speak of how and where to scatter him. We tossed out ideas while stuck in traffic, during television commercials, and whenever there was a lull in our conversation. We both liked the idea of finding a stretch of highway to ourselves, where my mother could step on the gas and I could pour my father out an open window.

But after debating buying big sunglasses and long skinny scarves and renting a shiny convertible, we realized the idea conjured images of a Sunday-night Hallmark television special. It took us a long time to settle on the obvious. Perhaps we avoided it because we knew the moment we began to discuss a plausible location, the event would become real. But the day I entered the closet and saw the cat sniffing at the edges of my father's box, I called my mother at work and asked, "What about the ocean?" My father had been happiest living in Santa Cruz with Steve. The Daddy I remember most fondly is the one strolling the boardwalk shirtless and running his fingers through his curls. I would tarry behind to collect driftwood chips and watch the eleven-foot-tall man make balloon animals. It's there I picture him smiling in the warm sun as Steve's hand slips into his back pocket.

Choosing a location should have been the easy part. By California law, it is illegal to spread ashes on public land; it is also a crime to spread ashes into the ocean from the beach. In fact, in federal ocean waters, law-abiding ash-spreaders must disperse their loved ones at least three nautical miles from shore. It is true that this law is often treated the way people treat jaywalking. But my mother is not a jaywalker. Neither did she intend to risk arrest while she said goodbye to a man who had caused her enough problems when he was alive.

While researching in the phone book, my mother and I were drawn to a charter business that, besides the standard fare of fishing cruises and private excursions for sweet sixteen and bachelor parties, offered what they called "Burials at Sea." Others offered similar services, but we liked that this company only had yachts, which we thought bestowed an element of class. We sought to avoid being just another sad sack of potatoes grieving for a loved one—entirely indistinguishable from the family that rented the boat the day before and the family that would rent it the day after. I wanted to stand on that boat and imagine that the night before a young man had sat on deck and received a lap dance while his buddies drunkenly cheered him on, something as unlike our real task as possible.

On the appointed day, at two in the afternoon, a man in a snug blue T-shirt with the name of the charter company in script across the front lumbered up to where we waited at a carousel. I held my father tightly against my chest. The man asked my mother if she was "the lady with the ashes," then introduced himself as Bill. He shoved his pawlike hand toward mine. I gripped my father tighter. As the three of us walked toward the boat, Bill talked, his belly jiggled, and he rubbed his bristled chin. I could see his lips moving, and I knew he was talking, but I couldn't hear him. This was a man who owned a tackle box and drank his liquor from a can. I had envisioned our yacht being piloted by a captain in a tailored navy blazer steering with one hand and holding a martini in the other, someone with whom my father might have shared a certain sensibility. The man before me was related to my father by anatomy only.

As we set sail for the open ocean, my mother swayed with nausea. "Here," Bill said, giving her a plastic bag. "In case you need to hurl." I faced the icy wind, watching the boardwalk fade until it looked as if the sky was down and water was up, and everything was a blue-gray haze. Bill cut the throttle, and we stilled, drifting in the waves. My mother joined me at the side of the yacht, and we opened the box containing my father. It felt to us as if we were opening more than just a box; we were opening him. I let my mother unfurl the plastic sack, and together we peered down at the pile of beige ash. She lifted the sack from the box, and we watched the wind pick my father up, crumb by crumb, until the dust of him was swirling above us like a kite. I thought of grade school and the puffs of chalk that billowed when you smacked the chalkboard erasers together, until finally the wind had taken my father away. As I watched him go, I was silent; there was no rage, no hysterics. I have never felt angry with him. I only wish his life had been easier, happier. I wish we could have known each other without the specter of death always looming over our relationship. It's what we never had that most makes my heart ache. Even the intimacy we had worked so hard to forge during my childhood seemed to float away that day along with his ashes.

On shore, Bill shook our hands. My legs did not trust the sand, the way it gave underfoot, and I wanted to be on the boardwalk. "You might want to stop in the restroom," Bill told us as we walked away. "Freshen up." We nodded dumbly. The afternoon crowd jostled us, knocking us together until my mother took my hand. We found a bathroom in a fast-food restaurant across the street and stood side by side at the mirror. Under the fluorescent light, my mother and I understood Bill's parting suggestion. Our faces—my mother's pale, mine flushed—were covered in a thin layer of ash, in what remained of my father. Silently, we dabbed wet toilet paper on our faces and arms until we were left with only ourselves.

22

THE SECOND TIME I WENT TO PARIS, I WASN'T alone.

But I wasn't with Ben, either.

He stayed home at our apartment on Grove Street. I know it's ours, because it looks nothing like it did when it was mine. When I lived there alone, its cleanliness intimidated my friends. Instead of sitting in my chairs, they merely hovered. Nobody ever brought red wine. I didn't care. My apartment wasn't for them or even for myself. It was for my father, and I made sure that my hardwood floors were always clean enough for licking.

Then Ben moved in, and I felt like even our spoons weren't clean enough for licking. I came home to clothes: crumpled boxers in the entryway and T-shirts under the dining room table. Food: brown apple cores on the living room rug and so many mugs with dried tea bags stuck to their insides. Gear: his bicycle blocking the front door and his sweaty yoga mat drying on the couch. Dirt: black footprints on the floor of the tub and something gummy on the drawer of the filing cabinet.

But I didn't panic until I saw Ben come in from a run and rub the sweat from his face with the dish towel I used to dry our dishes.

"What are you doing?"

"What? I'm wiping my face."

"But I use that towel to dry our dishes."

"You dry our dishes? You know they can dry on their own, right?"

"Why do you think it's called a dish towel? It's for *dishes*."

I took to planting a decoy dish towel on the kitchen counter and keeping a clean towel hidden in the cupboard, and I tried not to think of what that decoy went through when I wasn't there.

So Ben stayed home to defile our dish towels while I went to Paris with my mom. It was her sixty-second birthday and her first time in France. We arrived in the morning, dropped our luggage at the apartment we were renting, and set out for Jardin du Luxembourg. We circled the gardens before heading out toward Le Pantheon and beyond that to the Seine, L'Isle Saint Louis, and Notre Dame. All morning we kept to the Seine and the green booths where tan men sold old books, prints, and trinkets. We ate ice cream before noon and omelets after.

We walked everywhere until I realized, late in the afternoon somewhere near the Eiffel Tower, that I was walking by myself. I turned around. My mother was several feet back with one hand holding her side. I moved quickly toward her.

"What's wrong?" I asked.

"You're walking too fast."

"Sorry."

"I'm tired."

"I said I was sorry."

"Just wait until you're sixty-two. See how fast you move then."

I laughed. Good point.

"Do you want to stop? Get something to drink?"

My mom nodded.

"I want a real Coke," she said.

"A real Coke?" I asked.

"Not diet."

A street vendor sold us real Cokes and real snacks, and then we walked very slowly to the Eiffel Tower and decided not to climb the stairs. Instead, we found a bench and got sticky fingers eating inordinately expensive dried strawberries that had clearly been priced just for us—gullible tourists. We craned our necks up and watched our fellow tourists get smaller and smaller as they made their way to the top of Eiffel.

A young couple sat down on the bench next to ours with their daughter. She could walk and was probably close to three years old, but she still seemed a baby to me. We listened to their French, but the only thing that translated was the delight in their voices when they spoke to their little girl. She threw chip crumbs at pigeons and when they moved in close to feast, she galumphed toward them fearlessly, giggling as they skittered away. When the birds came back to finish the chips, she did it again. Again. Each time, she looked up at her parents for approval. She looked over at us, too, and when she did, we made funny faces, and she broke out smiling.

She lost interest in us after a while and we her. My mom and I continued talking, which is one of the things we do best, and I asked her something I'd never thought to ask before.

"When you were a kid, what did you want to be? When you grew up?"

She didn't hesitate.

"A mother."

My father had made her one.

I remembered this question from my own childhood when I'd given lots of different answers: news anchor, actress, librarian, waitress, Jessica Fletcher. About a year before my dad died, though, it started to bother me that I was always changing my mind. What was the common thread running through these professions? I decided that the only link was that, at different times, I thought all of them would make me happy. So that became my new answer: I told adults that when I grew up I wanted to be happy. I did that until my father told me to stop. He told me it was kind of a conversation stopper.

"So what did you want to be when you grew up?" I asked him.

He didn't hesitate.

"I wanted to be a black, female jazz singer."

I laughed.

"I did. When I was five. I didn't know I couldn't."

Then, I thought my father's ambition was funny and weird. Now, what I think depends on my mood. I always think it's funny. But, sometimes, I think it's also sad. My father may have been able to attempt a Michael Jackson in reverse and even get a sex-change operation, but he was never, ever, going to be able to sing jazz. Other times, it reminds me how fabulous my dad was. This story makes me love him even more. That's what he wanted to be, and it didn't occur to him it couldn't happen. All the doubt and fear and frustration and indignation came later. Of course I never knew my father when he was small and wonderful—full of wonder. But maybe it's enough to know he was that once.

There's a second tape. My father recorded it eighteen months before he died. He made it for me. It was late October, just before Halloween. I was Mona Lisa that year. I carried an empty gold frame out in front of me. My long dark hair was parted down the middle, and I wore a layered dress and shawl in shades of brown, gold, and burgundy. We even practiced the smile for days. But he wasn't satisfied. Something was missing. That's when he played Nat King Cole's song for me—"Mona Lisa."

He decided I should carry a recording of the song and play

it in the gym during the school Halloween parade and later, too, when I went trick-or-treating. So we recorded it on a portable tape recorder I could clip to my dress. But the tape doesn't begin with Nat. It begins with my dad: "Testing one, two, three. Testing one, two, three. Can it be heard at *this* distance? Can it be heard at *that* distance?" This or that. Tit or tat. On the tape, his voice is nasally and goes up slightly at the end of those two words, as if he were speaking Swedish or singing a nursery rhyme. You can hear him enjoying himself when he says them. I could listen to him say "this" and "that" over and over again forever. This recording is much shorter than his tape from Stockholm, only three minutes and change, and he's on it for less than thirty seconds. But I picture myself beside him, listening to him testing. I was there then, and I'm here now. This tape feels a part of me. There's no mystery. No question. I know what it's from. I know why it was recorded. It's not a clue. It's just a pleasant memory.

In Paris, I tried to summon the sound of my father's voice. I tried to hear him there beneath the Eiffel Tower. But I didn't have his tapes with me, and it'd been too long since I listened to either of them. Nor could I recall his smell or the pattern of veins on the back of his hands. Even if I could, they would only have been memories of someone who used to exist but did no more, nowhere. Memories alone would never be enough. Memories are like colors: they can be beautiful on their own, but they're so much more when they're used to make a painting. But what good is painting a painting if the person you want most to see it, never will?

On the bench beside my mother I felt something in my hair. My first reaction, I don't know why, was that it was a pigeon, and unlike the fearless baby, pigeons freak me out. I yelped and leapt up and away from the bench in a full-body shimmy that I hoped would frighten the pigeon as much as he had frightened me. Only, when I turned around, I realized there was no pigeon. It was just the girl baby standing behind our bench, her hand still outstretched. She wasn't smiling now, though. No, I'd made her cry. My mother reached to comfort her, but her father got there first, sweeping her up into his arms.

In my earliest memory, I'm three years old, and my parents and I are crouched behind a parked car after dark. It's December, and all around us houses are decorated for Christmas. But the obvious heart of the block is the home directly across the street from where we're hiding: it outshines the rest. Boldly colored blinking lights, rooftop reindeer, neon candy canes, sleighs and sleds, tinsel, snowmen, cartoon characters whose stories bear no Christmas connection, spinning pinwheels, glittery gift packages—it throbs with holiday spirit. Off to the side, almost in the neighbor's yard, is a life-size Santa Claus holding his list. Our dentist and her husband live in this house, and they are friends of my parents. Santa's list has only three names on it, my dentist's kids. But not for long.

I'm cowering behind the front tire. I turn to my parents, who are squatting beside me, and announce, "If we get caught, I don't know you." They shushed me and laugh, although they're trying not to. My father looks both ways and then scampers, back hunched, knees bent, across the street. My mother takes my hand, and we follow. I lean against a plastic puppy dog, lit from within. My mother opens a small can of black paint and tries to hand my father the paintbrush, but he's too busy measuring an even blank space on the list. "Louis. You're missing the point," she tells him. He hears her and takes the brush, lightly dipping it in paint. I watch my father write my name in thin black letters. When he finishes, we stand back to admire his work. I'm on the list, like I have three siblings and live in this big house with my big family.

But I don't. It's just a joke. My family is this man and this woman, who are running now, stooped and low to the ground, laughing. I run after them, following their laughter all the way home.

From the shadow of a white bird
Cling to the wings (background chorus)

I lived as a boy,
On a street named Paloma
A beautiful name for a dove
I grew to a man
On a street named Paloma
And lived life on the wings of love

Bye, bye, my blanco Paloma, bye, bye (background chorus)
Carry my dreams high on your wings
Fly through the sky to the heart of my child
Teach her songs she can sing

No tears for me, my Victoria
I'll always remain in your heart
Life is a dance, an incurable romance
Live yours as a work of art

Bye, bye, my blanco, Paloma, bye, bye (background chorus)
Carry my dreams high on your wings
Fly through the sky to the heart of my child
Teach her songs she can sing

I never knew I wanted a child
Never knew how to pray
An angel appeared as a blanco paloma
Answering unspoken prayers in the most beautiful way

No tears for me, my Victoria
I'll always remain in your heart
Life is a dance, an incurable romance
Live yours as a work of art

—Louis Loustalot

ACKNOWLEDGMENTS

Men may be the topic of much of this memoir, but it was a brigade of extraordinary women who willed this book into existence and whom I owe the greatest and deepest gratitude.

These are those women, and this is my thanks:

Alice Tasman, for her tireless literary guidance and savvy about all things life. I am incredibly lucky to have her in my corner.

Brenda Copeland, for deeming my writing worthy of her exceptional editing and me worthy of her exceptional friendship.

Patricia Fels, for making me believe I could be a writer. And for being one hell of a teacher.

Laura Chasen, for taking care of everything and always offering superb editorial advice. When Laura speaks, it's in your best interest to listen.

Stephanie Hargadon, for her enthusiasm, dedication, and publishing prowess.

Jessica Regel, Tara Hart, Laura Biagi, and Jennifer Weltz, for going to bat for me over and over again and doing it so well.

And Sally Richardson, for being an ardent supporter of my work and a badass role model.

In the midst of this female powerhouse, there are also two men who helped build this book. I thank:

Paul, for his wise counsel and faith in me.

Ben, for discovering the stack of career-change guides I checked out of the library and nudging me back into this lifestyle choice called writing. And for having the best heart of anyone I have ever known. That, too.